The Travels of Peter Mundy

The Travels

of

Edited by John Keast M.Ph BA (Hons)
Bard Gorhelwas
1950–1968

Peter Mundy

1597–1667

DYLLANSOW TRURAN

Dyllansow Truran
Cornish Publications
Trewolsta, Trewirgie, Redruth, Cornwall

First published 1984

*To my dear wife
who assisted with the text and illustrations
and whose ambition it is to travel with me
in the tracks of Peter Mundy*

Printed and bound in Great Britain by A. Wheaton & Co. Ltd., Exeter
ISBN 0 907566–75–8

PREFACE

Peter Mundy came from a merchant family settled for some years at Penryn in Cornwall. His father exported pilchards to France and Spain and it was intended that Peter should go into the family business. He was given a reasonably good education and then sent across the Channel to learn the French language. Subsequently he went to Spain and developed an ambition to travel to various parts of the world. He kept a journal of his several voyages and travels overland and when at home brought this up to date. Mundy may at one time have intended it for publication but was evidently content that it should be passed around his family and acquaintances – "to pleasure such Freinds that are Desirous to understand somewhat of Forraigne Countries."

A copy of part of the Travels was made in London in 1634 and came into the Harleian Collection at the British Museum (Harleian MS. 2286). The original passed to the Worth family at Mabe in Cornwall and then to the Rawlinson Collection at the Bodleian (Rawlinson MS. A 315). Both copies seem to have been almost forgotten until the early years of the present century.

In 1908 Lt. Col. Sir Richard Carnac Temple, Bart., C.B., C.I.E., who had recently retired from the Indian Army, commenced the lengthy task of transcribing and editing the Travels. As each volume reached completion, it was published by the Hakluyt Society and a full set is now comparatively rare. The work of Col. Temple and his assistants was carried out in a thorough and scholarly manner and every point which needed clarification was dealt with in a wealth of footnotes and appendices. The text was faithfully adhered to and the final work is in six volumes weighing about 10 pounds and containing nearly a million words.

To produce a version which I would like to think could be enjoyed by readers of all ages, I have taken considerable liberties with Peter Mundy's text, reducing it in length, re-arranging the order chronologically and replacing archaic wording and spelling. At the same time I have tried as far as possible to retain his vivid descriptive and narrative style.

JOHN KEAST

CONTENTS

LIST OF ILLUSTRATIONS

Some of the pen drawings made by Peter Mundy during his travels are reproduced at the end of certain chapters and captions to these appear on the pages concerned.

* The Battle of the Downs (pp 56–57) reproduced by kind permission of A.E. Raddy, Looe. All other illustrations reproduced by kind permission of The Mansell Collection.

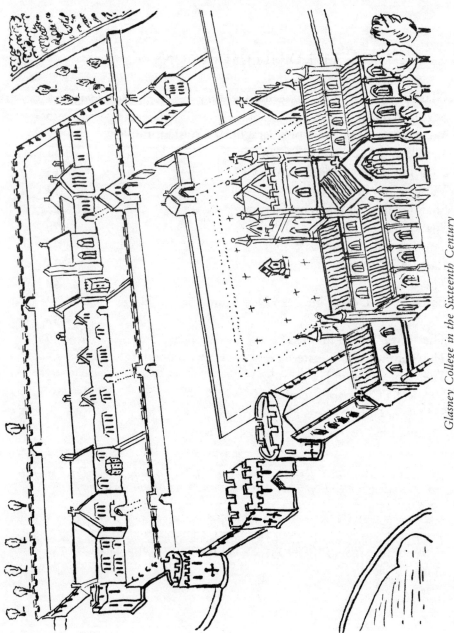

Glasney College in the Sixteenth Century

INTRODUCTION

Peter Mundy's family came from Penryn but had originated in Leicestershire. John Mundy came to London, prospered in trade and became Lord Mayor in 1495. His son of the same name followed in his footsteps and was chosen Lord Mayor in 1522. His fourth son, William, went into the Church, became a canon of Merton Abbey in Surrey and came to the notice of Prior Vyvyan who named him as his successor at Bodmin Priory in Cornwall. A great deal is known of Prior Mundy's business activities, particularly in the parcelling out of land belonging to the Priory to his friends and relatives. His brother John was granted a long lease of Rialton Manor near Newquay and his descendants held it until the Commonwealth. The Prior's nephew, William Mundy was married to Humphrey Prideaux's daughter whilst his brother John's daughter married Humphrey's son, William Prideaux.

Another member of the family, Peter Mundy was already installed as a canon at Glasney College in Penryn. His grandson, the traveller, was not sure whether he was a canon or a "chantoor", that is a singing priest – and there were certainly four choristers and three chantry priests on the establishment. It may well be that the grandfather instilled a lasting love and interest in music in the boy. When he was over sixty Peter Mundy deplored the loss of his lute-book whilst watching a procession in London. In 1548 it was the turn of Glasney College to be suppressed but it seems likely that Mundy had seen it all coming and already found a civil occupation at Penryn. There is very little real evidence but it is just feasible that of his four sons one at least started in the pilchard business. Penryn had trading connections with Fowey and William Mundy married Jane Withiel there in 1574 and became a merchant and innkeeper, who probably gave his name to Mundy's rocks at the harbour entrance. One of the Penryn family is mentioned in January 1594 as being concerned in a dispute with the men of Roscoff in Brittany. Five years later in a report dated 4 July 1599 Antony Mundy, merchant and owner of a small bark of Penryn is said to have arrived back from Rochelle bearing news of an engagement between French and Flemish ships and some

Spanish men-of-war off the coast of Brazil. Two years later, Robert Mundy reported to the authorities that he had met an Irishman just come ashore from a ship at Falmouth, who claimed that he was a nephew of the Bishop of Santiago and that he was carrying letters from Spain to Tyrone in Ireland. As a result of this information the man was held for questioning.

It is strange that the Cornish historian Hals who lived not so long after Peter Mundy makes no mention of him but Tonkin, writing early in the next century, maintains that our traveller was the son of Richard Mundy, senior of Penryn. If so, Robert Mundy may have been the uncle referred to, on whose behalf and that of his father, Peter acted as agent at Seville for the sale of their pilchards in 1621. The burial of Robert Mundy, merchant is recorded on the 16th October 1646. His daughter Joan married George Keast in 1625; their son Robert died an infant in the following year.

A daughter of John Mundy of Rialton married Hannibal Vyvyan whose sons Roger and Charles, travelled with Peter Mundy aboard the "Royal Merchant" to Constantinople. It is possible that Mundy had business connections with Samuel Enys of Penryn, who also lived for several years in Spain and like his compatriot managed to stay out of England during the Civil War returning at its conclusion to build up a prosperous business at home.

It seems likely that Mundy married during his stay at Penryn from 1647 to 1655. The registers of St Gluvias Church contain an entry under 1st March 1650 of the baptism of Peter, son of Peter and Ann Mundy and it may be conjectured as to what led to his deciding at the age of nearly 60 to embark on yet another voyage to India. He sailed from England in 1655 and returned three years later in time to witness the State funerals of Blake and Cromwell. After five years in London during which he recorded most of the events of the time but without betraying his sympathies for either King or Commonwealth, he decided to retire to Cornwall. Following a reference to the proclamation of the Treaty of Breda at Penryn in 1667 the journal comes to an end. It seems likely that Peter Mundy died at some time between 1667 and 1670: his burial is not recorded in the parish registers of St Gluvias.

CHAPTER I

Travels in France and Spain: The Mediterranean. From Constantinople to London.

1608–1627

From Penrin in Cornwall I passed with my father to Rouen in Normandy where we stayed one month and then returned home. This city lieth on the banks of the Seine. The river produceth a strange effect, called by us the Bore, especially at spring tide. This Bore comes suddenly many feet high, like great rolling, feathering waves, overturning small vessels and boats and all this of a sudden, appearing for a while like a tempestuous sea. There is at Rouen a great bell which I did not see but heard much thereof from others. It bears an inscription

"Je suis George de Granbois de cinquante mille poiz.
Mais qui me pesera, soixante mill me trouvera."

I heard a Dutch captain say that he measured the circumference and that it was 9 fathoms and a span. He being a tall man, it could not be less than 55 feet in circumference and about 30 tons in weight.

There are also many poor people, both men and women, sometimes a man and his wife, instead of horses, drawing small carts, transporting goods from place to place.

I was next sent to Bayonne in Gascony on the borders of France and Spain to learn the French tongue. There the artisans' wives wear an attire on their heads like unto morions or headpieces, made of linen, stuffed with cotton, coloured with saffron and stuck with pins. I was told they wear it as a reminder of their courage in assisting to expel the English about 1453. (Search the Chronicles) Servant maids keep their hair long, hanging down their backs and shoulders, but have the crown of their heads shaven like friars. Having remained here one year, I came home again in the year 1610.

3

On the 1st May 1611, I left my parents and went up to London with Capt. John Davis whom I served as cabin boy three or four voyages to San Lucar, Cadiz, Malaga etc and at length was left by him at San Lucar with Mr George Weaver, dwelling in the house of Senõr Pedro Patinno. At this place an Englishman married to a Spanish woman (and dwelling next door to us) killed his wife and one of the King's commissaries when he found them together. After some trouble, the Englishman was freed according to Spanish law. I stayed here two years and then was sent up to the city of Seville to stay with Mr Charles Parker.

Subsequently I visited Ayamonte and over to Castro Mareen and Travila in Portugal before returning to Spain where I lived for another two years and in that time made myself fluent in the Spanish tongue.

Of Seville much might be said, it being large, populous, rich and a place of great traffic.

The bridge over which they pass to Triana is built on great lighters, moored at both ends and rises and falls with the tide. The steeple or tower of the great church – La Giralda – is exceedingly high and built so that all 26 of the bells may be seen. The great bell is the best that ever I heard. The tower may be ascended on horseback until you come to the belfry. On the top of all is the image of a woman standing on a globe, holding a banner in her hand which is intended as a weather vane. This image is called La Giralda, from which the whole tower takes its name. From the tower I saw the high hills of Granada, reckoned to be 40 leagues distant. They are always covered with snow.

La Yglesia Mayor is the Cathedral of Seville and is admirably graced with rare and costly images and pictures and I believe, with the best music, both for instruments and voices in all Spain.

The Alcazar or King's House is also an elaborate structure. La Vega de Sevilla, or Valley of Seville is not to be paralleled for plenty, variety and excellency of its natural products, this part of Andalucia being considered the most fertile in all Spain. I had forgotten La Xarall de Sevilla which is a large forest of olive trees around the city, eighteen leagues about with many towns and villages. I was at the town of Las Dos Hermanas (The Two Sisters) for some time filling oil in pipes at the oil mills nearby.

From Seville I returned to London with Capt. Davis but I had

SEVILLE in SPAIN.

not been at home fifteen days before I was sent away again with Mr James Wyche, bound for Constantinople in "The Royal Merchant". In our passage we made calls at Gibraltar, Malaga, Alicante, Majorca, Minorca, Messina in Sicily, Xante, Scandarone or Alexandretta and Scio (Chios) near Smyrna. At almost all these places were English merchants by whom we were joyfully received and welcomed, our passage being very prosperous and full of various novelties and delights. The only scare was at Cape St. Vincent where the King of Spain's ships met with us at night. Each suspected the other of being Turkish pirates as there were reports of 26 sail being in the vicinity. But, God be praised, we parted friends.

Leghorn is the neatest, cleanest and pleasantest place I have seen, their houses painted outside with stories and landscapes in colour, making a very delightful show. Stromboli, near Sicily is a little round high island casting forth continual flames of fire and smoke not so well perceived by day as in the night, with such violence that it carrieth abundance of stone and ashes out with it. The stones falling into the sea are called pumice stones.

Scandarone or Allexandretta is the seaport for Alleppo, some three days journey distant. It is very unwholesome because the hills hinder the approach of the sun until nine or ten o'clock in the morning and it lies in a great marsh full of bogs, fogs and frogs. The tops of the mountains are always covered with snow and they abound with lions, wild boar, jackals and porcupines, of which last one was killed, brought aboard and roasted, proving very savoury meat.

We passed among the fruitful islands of the Archipelago and saw the place where Troy once stood. The mouth of the Black Sea is about 20 miles north of Constantinople where is a small island. To this place merchants resorted for recreation, myself also being there. At Constantinople the English merchants live very comfortably, with pleasure, love and amity and wear English dress. Fruit and wine are plentiful and in good variety. I remained here about three years but in the second year my master, Mr James Wyche, died of smallpox which usually visits this city every four or five years. So I remained with Mr Lawrence Green until the Honourable Sir Paul Pindar, the ambassador, was ready to return to England. The journey was to be overland and commenced on the

6th May 1620. There were 25 Englishmen in the company including myself, six Frenchmen and 21 Janissaries for protection. Sir Paul, the gentlemen and merchants were well mounted, the servants rode in the twelve waggons and 31 carts containing goods and baggage.

On the 12th May we arrived at the city of Adrianople but a terrible shower of rain, with thunder and lightning caused us to seek shelter in a great house belonging to the Grand Seigneur.

View of the Grand Signior's Seraglio at Constantinople

By the 20th May we had come to Sophia and were entertained by the local governor. After much salutation there was Sherbett brought in. It is a drink made of sugar, lemon juice and water, with which the better sort mingle amber, musk, roses, violets etc, this being the ordinary drink of great men, their law forbidding them wine; the poorer sort drink only water.

30th May. We came to the city of Belgrade lying on the Danube. Here my Lord (the ambassador) hired a house being determined to spend a few days: also our waggons were discharged, the plan being to use horses over the mountains. On the river in front of the city are 35 floating mills anchored by great baskets filled with stones. Each mill is built like a house on a great barge. The river is abundant in sturgeon, carp and pike which are sold cheaply. The city contains about 2,000 households, whereof 60 or 70 are Jews, the rest Christians and Turks. The Castle is worth notice being very much beautified with turrets, battlements and watchtowers and having within churches, baths etc: all the dwellers within are Turks and we were not suffered to enter the principal fort.

Very great boats are used to carry salt, wood and corn. The salt is digged out of the mountains in great pieces, blackish to sight, but being beaten small, exceedeth all other in whiteness. We likewise saw the Artillery House wherein were many brave pieces of brass ordnance which the Turks had lately taken from the Emperor, some dated 1596 to 1600.

The manner of these poor Bulgarians is that the men are generally labourers and clothed in white cloth: the women for the most part in russet. The virgins have their hair hanging down their backs, handsomely plaited: about their necks they have pieces of silver and brass, in their ears great earings of silver, some weighing a quarter of a pound. They go in their smocksleeves and barefooted.

The married women wear a linen cloth plaited over their tresses. At our passage through any village they would stand ready with hot cakes. Also milk, sweet and sour, fresh cheese, butter and eggs being brought to us by the youngest and prettiest wenches, and these, with the young women, holding hand and hand in a round, would dance and sing very merrily.

By a river by a stone bridge we found good ripe strawberries as none of our company ever saw the like: also many wild apple and cherry trees.

13th June.   We came to the city of Sarajevo which lyeth among the hills. The houses have their walls of clay, the roofs of timber. The people are very big and tall.

20th June.   Crossing over the river we dined under a Turkish garrison castle and came to another, lately taken from the Venetians, having yet their arms over the gate. And one mile beyond that is a stone marking the boundaries of the Venetian and Turkish dominions. We were no sooner past it but we entered into Christendom which seemed to us altogether a new world, such was the alteration we found not only in the inhabitants but also in the soil. Here the fields are well manured and in the midst of corn-fields, olives, pomegranates, pines and figs.

At our arrival at Spoleto (Split) we were conducted to a lazaretto, it being a custom that all travellers should abide here for a period before proceeding to Venice which they do to prevent infection. The traveller is first washed in the sea, afterwards with vinegar and then provided with another suit of clothes before he is allowed to take his passage by boat to Venice. My Lord hired a bark of ten tons and with a fair wind we passed by Zara, a garrison town where are 400 English soldiers.

3rd July.   Towards night, the wind coming fair, we set sail and by noon the next day came to the city of Venice. So passing between the two castles we came by St Mark's and to the Rialto bridge where we had to lower our mast to pass under. Lastly to Canalregio where we stayed and landed all our stuff at a house provided. This was most richly furnished with beds, hangings, tables all rich and curious, the chimney pieces of fine marble, being statues of gods and goddesses. Also a curious garden full of fine devices and marble images. The rent for two months was £20 and to Jews for hire of furniture and plate another £40.

27th July.   I went with a friend to see the famous Arsenal, a place about two miles in compass, walled around and with but one entrance for a galley to go in and out although there is space for two or three hundred to ride afloat. There are about a hundred great rooms open at either end for building new vessels and some were on the stocks. From thence to the place where they cast ordnance and to the great storehouse full of ordnance ready mounted on carriages. We were then shown where they made anchors, cables, ropes, oars, rudders, masts etc. Then we went upstairs where were halls hung with armour, swords, muskets, pikes and targets. In other halls were new sails ready made which are sewn by women. Then we were brought to the "Bucentaure" a vessel like a galley but shorter, thicker and higher, whereon is shown the ultimate in carved work overlaid with gold so that in the water she appears to be all gold. She hath two decks. On the lowermost sit the rowers and aloft sits the Doge himself in a stately seat and the Senators on each side. In this vessel goeth the Doge and nobility to marry the sea each Ascencion Day. The Doge letteth down into the water a rich ring and draweth it up at the end of the ceremony. Then they return with the greatest music and triumph, in company with other vessels. In this Arsenal there dwell only the Keepers; the workmen come in the morning and depart at night.

The Rialto bridge consists of one arch having two rows of dwellings on it with shops of several wares and trades. There is a multitude of gondolas, having tilts or awnings of black cloth with curious handsome seats. They are normally rowed or sculled by one man who stands upright near the stern.

4th August.   At three of the clock in the afternoon we came to the city of Padua.

11th August.   At evening we came to the great city of Milan.

18th August.   We began to ascend the mountain and entered into Savoy. The ascent may be about five miles and at the top is a fair clear lake.

21st August.   Shamberley – the fairest city we saw within the Alps, handsome comely buildings tiled with slates. All the towns we saw in the Alps (save this and St John's) were very poorly built; many of the poorer people had great wens under their chins.

24th August.   We came to the city of Lyons, great and populous: a place of great traffic, abounding with merchants and shopkeepers.

5th September.   Mr Davis, Mr Wilson and myself went to see the city of Paris; and first we saw one of the bridges over which we passed, not knowing but it was a street, having shops and dwellings on either side from end to end.

At the Louvre we saw a very rich hall, the walls of marble and

Venice in the Seventeenth Century

jasper, the roof richly gilt. There were divers statues of gods and goddesses of great antiquity. From thence to another large hall where were pictures of divers Kings and Queens of France.

Afterwards to the Exchange, it consisting only of a few shops where they sell bands, gloves, garters etc. And from thence to the great church of Notre Dame with two great steeples, one of which we ascended and saw the prospect of the whole city to our great wonder.

6th September.   Hired coaches from Paris to Calais at 40 crowns per coach.

11th September.   Unto the town of Marquise: we went along the seacoast in sight of England and came to Calais. Within the walls are nearly a thousand small cottages. At the gates, our guns were taken from us by the guards but in an hour's time returned to us at the Golden Head, kept by an Englishman. Here is but one church and a fair market place with a curious clock with small bells to strike the quarters, halfs and whole hours.

12th September.   There was a ketch hired to carry us to Dover but the wind over-blowing, they durst not venture over the bar.

13th September.   In the morning we departed from Calais and in three and a half hours arrived at Dover. We cast anchor near the town from whence a boat carried us on shore.

14th September.   Came to Canterbury. Here we went to see the Cathedral being goodly to behold.

18th September.   I came to London and lay in Mincing Lane at the house of Mr Richard Wyche.

20th March.   I went down to my friends in the country (Penryn) and at the end of that summer I made a voyage to Seville in Spain with pilchards on the account of Mr Richard Wyche, my uncle and my father.

22nd April 1622.   After my return from Spain I covenanted with Mr Wyche to serve him five years, on certain conditions.

15th April 1625.   By my said master and others (undertakers of a contract with the King of Spain's commissioners for a great quantity of copper to be delivered in Spain at a certain price and at certain set times) I was sent post over thither with one Henry Davis.

We departed from London on Saturday night and lay at Gravesend. Next day to Dover. On Monday we crossed over to

Paris in the Seventeenth Century

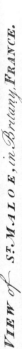

VIEW of ST. MALO E, in Britany, FRANCE.

Dieppe and the Sunday following were at Irun in northern Spain, having had good roads, good horses, fair weather and short stages. We usually exchanged 18 to 20 horses a day and occasionally 21 or 22, a very painful employment to one not accustomed to it, for the first two or three days. In my opinion there is better accommodation for post riding in this Kingdom (and more frequently used) than in any other place.

From Irun we came to Vitteria, a city in Castile where I found Mr George Wyche, my master's brother tied down because of legal difficulties with the contract. This place is one of the most delightful and hither retire lords and grandees from the tumult of Court to refresh and recreate themselves. Here is a very fair river, pleasant and artificial fountains, groves of trees, the best fruits and the fairest Plaza, built four square in unity upon pillars of stone in which at festival times, they bait their bulls with men, run their horses etc, on Corpus Christi days.

Here I remained about four months and then returned to San Sebastian to take my passage in the "Margett", Mr Robert Moulton, for England. Here I found my master very sick of the dropsy and shortly afterwards he left this life and I went down to my friends in Cornwall by land.

Having remained a while at home I made a voyage to St Malo in Brittany, a place of very great strength and traffic, there being the most fairest and biggest shipping of any port in France.

Women's head-dress. Peter Mundy's own sketches made at Bayonne.

CHAPTER II

First Voyage to India

1628–1634

A Journall of a Voyage made in the Good Shipp Expedition burthen 350 tunns, Thomas Watts, master, in Companie of the Jonah, burthen 800 tunns, both bound for Surat in East India.

6th March 1627 [1628]   Our Shipp weighed from Blackwall, and that night shee Anchored at Gravesend.

24th March 1628.   About this time I came down to Deal with some of the [East India] Committee, they coming to speed the Ships out of the Downs.

27th March.   We set sail out of the Downs.

30th March.   We saw Rame Head: much rain and so much wind that we took in both our topsails and spritsails. This day we saw two ships, the one a man-of-war of Flushing, the other a Brazilman, her prize, with 700 chests of Sugar.

31st March.   At two in the morning we set our topsails again. At six we saw the Lizard. This day we spoke with 4 shipps, the "Abigall" (Admiral), the "Charitie" (vice-admiral) and in them the two Captain Kirks and Capt Hutchens in a Pinnace, these three bound for the Azores and the "Blessing", Capt Morris bound for Madeira.

16th April.   We past among the Canary Islands and saw the peak of Teneriffe in my opinion the highest hill in the world, at least that I have seen.

21st June.   Pintados seen, spotted all over white and black.

During this voyage to Surat, taking into consideration our prosperous, healthy and pleasant passage out we determined to make a collection, levied at the rate of two pence in the pound out of every man's wage to the Hospital at Blackwall, a godly and religious work lately begun by the Honourable East India Company. A total of £186 was subscribed.

In crossing the line, the heat tolerable, little cold. We saw divers whales of the common sort, three or four together playing about our shipp. Also a great fish called a Shovell-mouthed whale and a great number of flying fishes. We caught divers sorts including Grampus, Porpoise, Albacore, Bonitoes, Dolphins, Pilot fish and strange sea fowl, among the rest a Booby which lighting on our yards allowed itself to be taken with mens' hands. The Shark is a very daring, ravenous fish, by report he often siezes on men and boys as they are swimming. It is often accompanied by small pilot fishes and little sucking fishes.

3rd July.   This day we saw land and made it to be the Cape of Bon Esperansa or Good Hope. We put not in by reason all our Men were in very good health.

26th July.   We saw the great Island of Madagascar.

Madagascar is held to be one of the greatest islands yet discovered. The people are black, well proportioned, strong limbed, active, tractable and sociable with us: the hair of their heads is made into little plates hanging round about and some have part thereof bound upright on the crown, which they anoynt with butter, oyle or grease. We bartered with them, cornelian beads for bullocks: these beads they esteem and offer for them pieces of gold or gold rings with precious stones in them. So that for seven or eight of these beads, scarce worth 7d each in India, we could have a bullock worth £3 or £4 in England.

We stayed at Mohilla, one of the Comoro Islands, two or three days, a very pretty, pleasant and fruitfull island, full of shady woods of strange trees, springs and little rills of water.

Great Comoro is a huge massy island but our Shipps never touched there by reason of the treachery of the inhabitants.

The wind and weather were fair when we left Mohilla and we could have arrived at Swally fifteen or twenty days earlier. Instead we were forced to shorten sail because of the Company's order that no ship should approach before the end of September when the rains begin to cease. Until that time the foul weather and strong currents are very dangerous to shipping.

28th September.   Mr John Willoughby and myself went in the "Jonah's" barge from Valentine's Peak with the Company's letters to advise of our approach and to see how matters stood in these parts between the Portuguese, the Dutch and ourselves.

30th September.   I arrived at Surat where were many English merchants by whom I was friendly welcomed. The same day our ships came in to Swally and thus, by God's permission, we came to our desired port, having been six months and three days from the time of our sailing from the Downs.

Events since my arrival at Surat in September 1628 till my departure for Agra in November 1630.

After my settling on shore at Surat, I was employed to write in the office, as newcomers usually are, unless they be men of rank.

The house we live in at Surat is one of the best in the town, being strongly built with a flat roof which no rain can penetrate. Below there is a fine hall with chambers and rooms for the President and members of the Council. The merchants have complete ware-houses and there is a large garden with walks round it and covered with vines supported on trellis work. In the middle is a pretty room, covered overhead, where you may sit and pass the time. In front is a little tank for washing in time of heat and rain. In this house dwelleth the President and his Council, merchants and under-factors numbering from ten to twelve, a preacher and surgeon, steward and attendants as well as cooks, bakers and serving men – in all 25 or 26 Englishmen.

Our food is for the most part such as we have in England, fine wheaten bread, beef, mutton, hens and pigeons dressed by our English cooks. Sometimes we have local wild fowl, antelope and occasionally wild boar but usually we have dopeage (dopyaj) and rice and pickled mangoes. Our strong drink is Racke like strong water, next a kind of beer made of coarse sugar and other ingredients, pleasant to the taste and wholesome – but mainly plain water.

The Factories which come under Surat, besides Persia, are Agra, Ahmadabad, Baroda, Broach and sometimes Cambay. In each place there are normally residing a Principal, with three or four Factors. Being very well accommodated and well furnished with everything that rich and fruitfull country affords, they live very contentedly together.

Surat lies on the river Tapti about twelve miles eastward from Port Swally. There are seven gates. One is the Baroche Gate out of which goe many an Englishman who never returns, for it is the road to our place of burial. There are some long straight streets, some fair buildings and a strong Castle with good ordnance. There is a spacious green called Castle Green and the bund or wharf where goods are loaded for transhipment into vessels or junks riding at anchor at Port Swally or the river mouth. These local junks have only one deck and some may be of 1,000 or 1,200 tunns each. They put to sea with the easterly monsoon and before the wind, out go our ships, by reason of the monstrous breadth of their mainsails and their confidence in the continuance of fair winds and weather during that monsoon.

What a monsoon is. Monsoon is a time of the year when the winds blow continually one way. There are two.

The easterly begins about the end of September and continues until the middle of the following April, with almost perpetual fair weather. The westerly monsoon lasts from the middle of April to the end of September and in the last three months the rain falls accompanied with great storms: there is no putting to sea and vessels are hauled on shore.

The great tank (or reservoir) at Surat is artificially made to store rainwater and is nearly half a mile around. It is for common use and there are entrances for people and cattle. Before the rains come, whilst the water level is very low, the floor is used for sowing musk and water melons which reach maturity very quickly. Round about stand many fair tombs, gardens and trees, whither we often resort for recreation.

At Surat lives Mr John Leachland an Englishman who was at one time in the service of the East India Company. For the love of an Indian woman, by whom he had sundry children he decided not to return to England when his time expired. Because of the great mortality the Company were glad to make use of his services although he was no longer in their employ. The Englishmen here sometimes visit his house to pass away the time.

Now before I take leave of Surat I will relate one accident that happened whereof I was eye-witness, that is a Banian woman that voluntarily burned herself alive with the body of her dead husband, after getting leave from the Governor.

A Journey from Surat to Agra.

11th November.   We departed from Surat in the evening and
soon met with Mirza Mahmud Safi, a Persian unto whom the
President had recommended us for our better safety and accommodation in so hazardous a time: for a great famine had begun and
the highways were becoming almost impassable for thieves and
others intent on stealing food and grain instead of riches.

30th November.   We came to the city of Burhanpur where we
stayed five days. Here is a fine castle standing on a hill overlooking
the river in which is an elephant cut in stone and coloured so that
from a distance it looks alive.

6th December.   Having taking leave of Mirza Mahmud Safi,
rendering him many thanks for our kind usage, we left him and
departed.

25th December 1630 and Christmas day.   We came to this place
(Kulharas) after passing through country rich in corn. This day a
messenger arrived from Agra. At our manzul or resting place we
fell to our Christmas cheer. The main dish was called Roast Beef
but the truth is that it was a piece of buffalo, both hard and tough
and a trial for our jawes and digestion but we did have a cup of sack
wherewith to remember our friends. We were much beholden to
Capt. Moreton who produced some English salt pork and neats
tongues for which the dogs pestered us. But our servants being
Muhammadans, would not so much as touch it.

30th December.   We came to Gwalior, a town adorned with
fair stone gates and houses supported with stone pillars. But the
Castle above all is to be admired, being a work of magnificance and
gallant prospect. The wall round about well kept and repaired full
of battlements and turrets.

3rd January.   We arrived at the city of Agra, the imperial seat
of the Great Mogul, our much longed for place of repose and with
much joy were received by our loving friends, Mr William
Fremling and Mr Crispen Blagden, about three miles out of the
city. Then we met Mijnheer Voorkneckt, the Dutch factor and
together we went to the Mogul's garden and having refreshed
ourselves there, came to the English house. Here we passed three
or four days entertaining our friends and then applied ourselves to
the Company's affairs.

The river Ganges.   At the place where I passed over, the river is about seven or eight fathoms deep, the water dark green. In time of rains, it overflows the banks to a distance of eight or nine miles. The Hindoos report a thousand fables of it and come as many miles to wash themselves clean of their sins. I passed to the farther side in a boat but swam back, it being not very broad.

25th December 1631.   I returned to Cole wherein a few days I bought, weighed, filled and skinned forty great bundles of indigo and ordered my servants to convey it to Agra as I had to go to Shergath about the Company's saltpetre lying there.

18th August.   This day, sitting on my cot, five or six carters, being Hindoos, came to dress their meat just to windward of me, so that the smoke blew right into my face, whereof being told three or four times and no notice taken. I took up a tent pin and flung it at their pot which fell into the fire. They then retrieved the contents which they gave to their oxen. Now my hand touching the pin, the cowdung and fire, the fire the pot and the pot the meat that was in it, it was just as if I had actually handled their meat, which was abominable to them. In the end I had to give them money to buy more meat.

6th August 1632.   I departed from Agra and came to Nut Mahal's market where eight carts laden with quicksilver, vermillion etc were delivered into my charge [the Company had unwisely imported large quantities of these materials expecting a quick and profitable sale: it was now left on their hands and the factors had the unenviable task of making as much money as they could out of the unwanted commodies.]

27th August.   We came to Allahabad. [The Indian merchants would only bargain for small quantities]. In the end Mundy was left with three alternatives – to return with the goods, to store it locally in several repositories in the hope of a future sale or to sell the whole for whatever price he could obtain.]

21st October.   I concluded for the whole, selling the quicksilver at Rupees 3½ per Sere and the vermillion at Rupees 4 per Sere unto 40 shopkeepers.

Patna.

This city lies along the river Gangees extending with its suburbs for three miles: there is a very long bazaar with trees on each side.

It hath more than two hundred grocers or druggists. It is the greatest market for all this country. The Hindoos of this place ferry all their dead over the river and there burn them.

30th November. We crossed the river Gangees which I proved to be about two arrows' flight over as I made trial from about the middle of it with my bow and arrows.

Description of the Great Mogul's coming from Burhanpur unto his Garden called Darreecabaag and so to Agra.

1st June 1632. Myself with Sundar Das went to see the Mogul's coming thither. Before we could get out of the city we were stopped and hindered by a great number of elephants, camels, carts and coaches. The coaches are generally drawn with oxen and hath but two wheels. A palanquin is a thing to be carried on mens' shoulders, six or eight at a time. Dowlees are similar but carried by only two men, wherein only one person may conveniently sit cross-legged, commonly employed for women closely covered.

We overtook the Governor of Agra who was going out to meet and do reverence to the Mogul. Behind him certain great elephants with flags, then some light camels who are used to be sent on matters of haste. Then 60 or 80 other camels, each carrying one gun. We went forward, meeting with a multitude of elephants and camels laden with tents, chests and bedding. Then about 160 elephants carrying on their backs howdahs, close covered, some with red, others with green and blue colours. Then 20 coaches and then thousands of horsemen, then 19 or 20 great elephants of state with coverings and furniture; most of them of cloth of gold; the rest of rich stuffs, velvet etc. some of them carrying a flag with the Mogul's arms which is a tiger crouching with the sun rising over his back. Then came the Mogul himself mounted on a dark grey horse and with him Mahabat Khan riding side by side. A little distance behind rode Dara Shikoh, his eldest son, all alone. All the rest of the lords on foot, before and behind and on each side of him. A good space off came the armed retinue, being a mighty army of horsemen, their lance-heads glittering brightly in the sun. Then a great number of elephants which seemed like a fleet of ships, with flags and streamers belonging to the great lords. Then the common people without number. And in this manner the

Shah Jehan Walking in his Garden

Great Mogul came to his Garden where he remained until the 10th June and then about midnight was brought in a palanquin to his Castle of Agra two miles distant.

Of Agra.

Agra is situated on the river Jamna. The Castle and the great mens' houses on the one side and their Gardens on the other side yielding a most delectable prospect. It is very populous by reason of the Great Mogul's keeping of his Court here: such a number of elephants, horses, coaches, soldiers etc that is incredible: in the Bazaar there is such a throng that men can hardly pass. To encompass all would take at least 14 or 15 miles. Here is a College of Jesuits with three or four padres; also Christians that have pay from the Mogul; a Venetian goldsmith, a French embroiderer and a physcitian. Places of note are the Castle, Akbar's tomb, the Taj Mahal, the Gardens and Bazaar.

The Castle stands on the river side, built of square hewn red stone. By the river the walls lie straight for a quarter of a mile and then curves round to the city. Here is the best prospect with battlements and the roofs of the Mogul's residence, some overlaid with gold. The gates and posterns are many: the entrance to the Bazaar has on each side an elephant in stone. Nearby another entrance lie many large pieces of ordnance.

Akbar's Tomb is two miles from Agra, standing in a great garden with four great gates. One excels all others I have seen in India having two very high spires. From hence is a long walk to the mausoleum itself which is four square, lessening towards the top, having several galleries adorned with cupolas. In the middle stands a tombstone in the shape of a horse, of solid marble, curiously wrought.

The Great Mogul is now building a sepulchre for his late deceased consort whom he dearly loved, having had by her nine or ten children. There is already about her tombe a rail of gold. The building is begun and goes on with excessive labour and cost, gold and silver being used like common metal and marble as ordinary stone.

The gardens around Agra are many, usually being square and enclosed with a brick wall and towers. In the middle is the chief house of pleasure and tanks, some of great capacity. The various

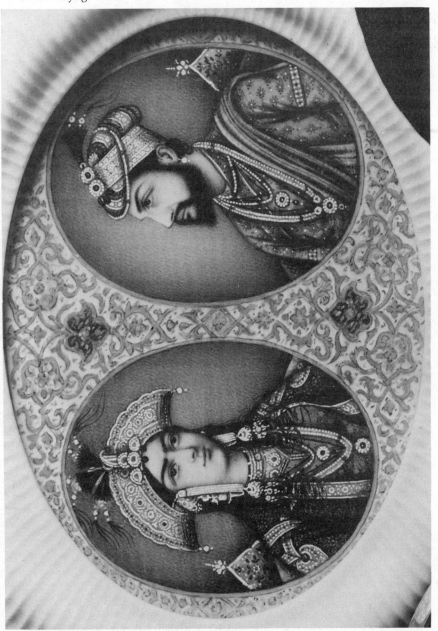

Shah Jehan and Mumtaz Mahal

walks are flanked with cypresses and beds contain apple trees (these scarce), orange, mulberry, mango, coconut, fig, plaintain trees. In other beds are your flowers and herbs: roses, marigolds and French marigolds in abundance; red poppies and white carnations, and divers other sorts of fair flowers which we know not in our parts – all watered by hand in time of drought which is nine months in the year. The carved work of perforated red stone is much used in all their gardens and tombs. In a building in one garden were many painted rooms copied from European prints which they value. Also there was a picture of Sir Thomas Roe, late ambassador here.

The Bazaar affords plenty of beef, mutton, partridge, quails, pigeons, turtle doves and sometimes geese and ducks; mangoes, plaintains and pineapples; raisins, almonds, pistachios, walnuts, apples, oranges, prunes, prunellas or dried apricots.

The Honourable East India Company has a house here, a quiet place in the heart of the city where we live according to the custom of the country. The rooms in general are covered with carpets with great round high cushions to lean on: we sit on the ground at our meat or discourse. Our dress when we go out is a turban on our heads, a white linen scarf over our shoulders; then a fine white linen coat, a girdle to bind about us, breeches and shoes, our swords and daggers by our sides. But when we go out in the country we have our bows and arrows by our saddle and a buckler hanging on our shoulders. However, we never stir a foot out of doors but on horseback, this being the custom of the country.

A Journey from Agra to Surat with a Caravan consisting of 268 camels and 109 carts laden with 1493 fardles of indigo and 12 fardles of saltpetre etc under the conduct of Peter Mundy, with a company of 170 soldiers.

25th February 1635. We set out from Agra in the morning with several friends, English, Italian and Dutch and having sat for a while by a tank a mile outside the city which is the usual place of parting, they returned to Agra and I went on my journey.

26th February. About noon we had much thunder and wind with such a deal of dust (which is usual at Agra before the rains) that we could scarce see one another. After this followed abund-

The Taj Mahal at Agra

ance of rain which accompanied us to Neemba where we pitched
our tents for that night.

27th February. About noon there was such a tempestuous
shower of rain mingled with hail that the like hath seldom been
seen. It lasted near half an hour.

22nd March. The way stony as it is in some places in Cornwall, being of the kind of stone which we call moor stone. Good
hunting for five hares were chased by the people to and fro. There
were also many fields of poppy, of which they make opium, much
used for many purposes. The seed of the white poppy they put on
their bread. Of the husk they make a beverage which is inebriating.
In like manner they use a certain plant called bhang having the
same effect so that you may have an opium eater, an opium drinker
or a drugtaker (bhangi).

24th March. Trees scarce all the way. A few poor towns
environed with thorn hedges to keep out thieves. The inhabitants
generally Rajputs. There is scarce one part in a hundred cultivated,
the rest lying desert and waste.

3rd April. This day my curiosity led me to see one of the
craggy hills on whose top there appeared to be a high tower.
Passing over rocks, clefts and dangerous places, here was the true
pattern of a fearful desert place. Men I saw none, only owls, wild
peacocks, foxes, hares, wild cats etc and not a drop of water to be
found. I got up with much labour, leaving behind fragments of my
torn apparel on thorns and bushes. On the very top stood a huge
stone, appearing from afar off like a mighty high tower. As we
returned we heard whooping and calling and when we were come
to our tents, we were told there were about sixty of our men out
looking for us.

25th May 1633. About nine o'clock we came to Variao and I
with some other English came to Surat to the English factory
where I made an end of my tedious journey from Agra.

At my arrival there were but few living of those I left here at my
departure, the rest dead from the sickness that followed the
famine. The like time was never seen in India, there being scarce
one man in the factory able to set his hand to paper. The famine
alone swept away more than a million of the poorer people.

14th November. By the Presidents' order I was appointed
Factor at the Marine. So departed from Surat and came to Swally
and there received all European goods now come with the newly

arrived ships. Soon after, my time being expired, I was permitted to take passage in the "Mary" for my native country.

A Journal of a Voyage from Surat to England in the Shipp "Royal Mary", capt. James Slade. God prosper it.

1st February 1634. We weighed (anchor) from the outer road of Swally in company of the "Jonah", "Palsgrave", "Hart", and "Discovery" bound for the Persian Gulf and the "Reformation" and pinnace "Intelligence" for Sumatra.

2nd February. There came to us three Malabar frigates. The captain in charge came aboard us and agreed with our English merchants that we should be allowed to go to Bhaktal to load pepper. In the meantime they put aboard of us 31 bags of pepper weighing about one cwt each, and we gave him a small brass gun.

21st February. We saw two sail, probably Portuguese carracks bound home, but we had no great mind to speak with one another.

22nd March. We passed near the island of Mauritius. Some part of it is high land, the rest plain. Great store of goats, hogs and some bullocks. Dodoes, a strange kind of fowl, twice as big as a goose, that can neither fly or swim, being cloven footed; a wonder how it should come thither, there being none such in any part of the world yet to be found. I saw two of them that had been brought to the factory at Surat. Also a fowl called Mauritius hens: if one is captured, the rest will come around you so that you may catch them alive with your hands. Great store of very great tortoises which are excellent meat as are their eggs. In conclusion it is a dainty island of good refreshing for homeward bound ships. It is now yearly frequented by us and also by the Dutch homeward bound. There is also great store of ebony growing there.

13th May. This day we anchored in Saldanha (Table) Bay.

This is that road where ships, outward and inward bound, put in for water, and in former times exchanged beef and sheep for iron hoops, pieces of copper etc. There have been lions often met with here but we saw none. On the shore great bones of whales and a number of seals. Ostriches have been seen by some, their eggs making good meat.

The people here are swart in colour and have very little or no beards, being also without any religion, law, art or civility that we could see.

Near the road are four notable places — the Table, the Sugar Loaf, Charles Mount and James Mount. The Table is a very high mountain, level at the top: the most part of it is a perpendicular rock. Myself and two others went up by a great opening like a valley but wondrous steep, the rocks on each side like monstrous walls from which there exudes water constantly. We were fain to pull ourselves up by the rushes and long grass. Aloft we found it like a plain down, many great flat stones lying around. There came a cloud towards and enclosed us, we being as it were in a great mist: it passed quickly away, leaving us a little wet. So having left a token of our being there (three stones) we returned. We went up about one o'clock and returned by eight at night. Table mountain is never without clouds but in fair weather. When it is covered in cloud, rain and bad weather are in the offing.

Next is the Sugar Loafe. At the top I found sundry reminders of Englishmen as "Thomas Lukins" "S.W.1630" etc. carved in stone. On the top is a quoit. I managed to climb on to the top, the rest of the company staying below.

At our coming into the road we saw fire on Penguin Island but as the wind was contrary could not land there until we were ready to proceed on our voyage. The master and myself went to the island and found Hadda, a native, in charge. He had been carried to Bantam in an English ship (the "London") and then brought back to Penguin island where he now lived with his family and friends numbering 60 in all. Hadda was dressed completely in English clothes. He spoke a little English and handed over letters which Capt Pyne had left on his departure for England. The little colony lived in seven little cottages in a row, with the cows, pigs, hens and chickens given to them by Capt. Pyne. We would have gone to see them but had not the time as our ship was now approaching under sail.

11th June.   We anchored at St Helena, a quarter of a mile from the shore close under the hills. During the time of our stay here, the Captain allowed the people to go ashore in parties and remain three or four days refreshing themselves with what they caught and killed, sending part aboard. All the time we lay becalmed and in smooth water very secure.

27th June.   We saw Ascension and put by it. This island is accounted bigger than St Helena but it is very bare and nothing to be had there but seafowl and fish. No ship would willingly touch there unless it has overshot St Helena.

July.   A man fell overboard but getting hold of a jointstool thrown over to him, he was hauled into our jolly boat in spite of rough weather.

25th August.   We saw a ship at which we rejoiced, hoping to speak with her to get news of our friends in England and also to get refreshment for our sick men, there being 40 down with a kind of swelling like dropsy. But she would not come near us although we used all possible signals, putting out our Colours, striking our top gallant sails, hoisting and lowering our foretopsails, shooting off two pieces of ordnance but all in vain.

26th August.   We saw two other ships steering right towards us. They were the "Griffin" and the "Phillipp" bound for New England. Our master and myself went on board the former in which were 200 people, mainly passengers, men, women and children bound for the plantations. The captain would gladly have spared us some beer but the seas were so high that we could not have got it aboard. With so many passengers and so long a voyage there was nothing else which could be offered to us.

5th September.   We spoke with two barques of Plymouth who supplied us with poor John (dried hake) bread, hens etc. This day we had sight of the Scilly Isles and we also buried Goodman Wilson, our Smith.

6th September.   We spoke with Sir Charles Pennington in the "Charles" and the "Garland"; also the "Tenth Whelp" who supplied us with good beer, peas etc.

7th September.   We spoke with the "First Whelp" of whom we also got some refreshing. This night John Gee fell overboard and could not be saved, it being dark and the ship moving at great speed.

8th September.   We spake with a ship from Lisbon from whom we had some lemons for our sick men.

9th September.   We came before Dover and were there put on shore.

10th September.   About two in the afternoon we took post horses and by six in the morning we arrived in the City of London.

CHAPTER III

A Journey to London by Way of Weymouth and Portland. By Pleasure Boat down the River Thames.

1634 to 1635.

Some Observations since my arrival home from India 1634

Having cleared with the Honourable East India Company, I prepared to go down to my friends in the country but in the meantime I was invited by Mr Thomas Barlow (who returned with us in the "Mary") to view some rareties at John Tradescant's, so went with him and another friend where we spent that whole day examining and that superficially, such as he had gathered together, as beasts, fowl, fishes, serpents and worms: precious stones, corns, shells and feathers of sundry nations, curiosities in carving and painting etc, as 80 faces carved on a cherry stone, medals etc. Moreover a little garden with divers outlandish herbs and flowers being supplied by noblemen, gentlemen, and sea captains with such curiosities as they could bring or procure from other parts.

Also at Sir Henry Moody's in the Strand, one of his gentlemen showed me divers inventions of his master. Among the rest, the room being quite dark, only one little hole in it with a glass through which a light was directed on to a sheet of white paper on the opposite wall and there was represented, as in a mirror all that was going on outside, as boats rowing on the Thames, men riding on the other side etc, but all reversed or upside down in their true colours.

Not long after I went to the Tower of London where I saw a Unicorn's horn about 1½ yards in length and 2 to 2½ inches at the bigger end, going taperwise and wreathed, although somewhat smooth, I think by often handling. It was white, resembling the substance of an elephant's tooth, estimated to be worth £18 or £20,000. This, as all the rest are, conceived to be rather the horn of

32

some fish than of a beast, because such a beast now is not to be found, although discoveries at present are in far greater perfection than they were then.

Being safely arrived and welcomed home by my friends (in Cornwall) after a few days I returned to London to sell some Indian commodities that would not sell in the country and took my passage in a lobster boat. There are two of them which regularly come and go to the Westcountry to take away lobsters which have been bought from local fishermen and kept in pots until they arrive. Each boat may carry about 100 dozen and in one summer 14 or 15,000 lobsters at least. They wait until the wind is fair and then lay them on the ballast in the hold. Within 48 hours they are at Weymouth but what with being in the boat and on horseback before they arrive at London, nearly a third are dead and must be sold cheaply. The royal kitchens are first supplied and then the Court and City.

Some four or five miles to the eastward of Falmouth we stopped at The Gull Rock, there to take in some crabs. Here do resort to breed sea fowl such as Gannets, Gulls, Seamews, Shags etc which belong to a country gentleman who from time to time takes away their young. At the approach of anyone there is such a fearful confused noise of different kinds of fowl, old and young, with multitudes hovering and fluttering in the air that it is strange to see and hear. By contrary winds we put into Torbay but next morning we departed and so arrived at Weymouth. Having occasion to stay a day or two I went to the peninsula of Portland, about two miles from the town. At Abbotsbury are bred many Swans, the royalty of which belongs to Sir George Strangwayes who dwells nearby. They have their wings pinnioned to prevent their flying away. They breed among the sedge on the shore. There come divers wild ones among them and in winter all sorts of waterfowl flock there.

Now back to Portland. There are two castles, one named Portland Castle and the other Sandfoot Castle which command the Roads and landing places. Off Portland is the Race which is avoided by seamen because of the tumbling, rippling, tempestuous swelling waves.

Then I went to the hewers of stone, some of which is used in repairing St Paul's Church in London. There were about two hundred workmen, some hewing out of the cliff above, some

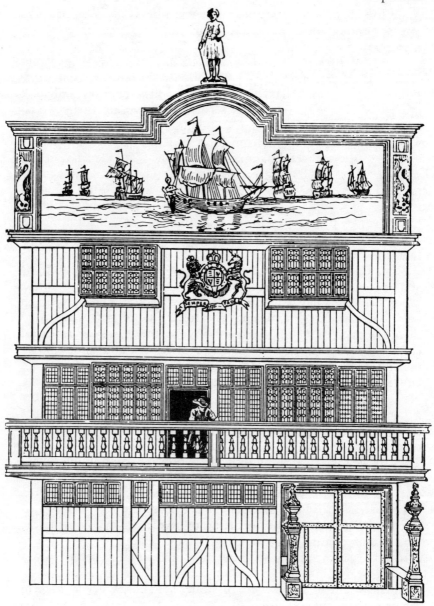

East India House

squaring, some carrying down, some loading. Some stones were already squared and weighed 9, 10 or 11 tons.

For fuel they use cowdung, kneaded and tempered with short straw and made into flat cakes as they do in India. Here I saw a black fowl with yellow bill and legs commonly called Cornish daws, which I never before saw out of that county. Portland oysters, found only in one parish, are much esteemed. When I returned to Weymouth I found on the grass a multitude of small coloured snails, half as big as peas. The people report that they drop out of the air, finding them on their hats as they walk in the fields. The like is reported of the raining of small frogs in the Isle of Jersey. From Weymouth I went to Dorchester passing a place called Maiden Castle, a work of great labour; some monument of the Danes or Saxons' fortification.

Having ended my business in London I returned to the country to see Basing House, the most part built at excessive cost of brick but now forsaken and desolate. From thence I went to the ancient city of Winchester. Here in the old Castle is a great Hall and at one end is fixed aloft King Arthur's Round Table. In the Cathedral Church were sundry tombs including the bones of Queen Emma and divers other noblemen and prelates whose bones were lately taken up and placed aloft in little ricks or chests about the Chancel.

I had not been long at home (Penryn in Cornwall) but becoming tired of being unemployed and because of the draining away of money and other reasons I resolved to return to London to look for a voyage which would fill the time as well as provide for the future. I arrived there at the end of November 1635 and found two options open, a voyage to India with the East India Company and another with a fleet setting forth by Sir William Courteen upon an unknown design and this latter I decided upon which God prosper.

In the meantime Sir William's son being about to take his passage in a small vessel called the Pleasure boat of about seven tons down to Woolwich to see if the ships were ready for sea, I was invited to go with him. The boat is fitted for speedy sailing and most of the space aboard is taken up with a great Cabin, fitted with table, carpet, benches and cushions: with windows which open and shut, painted within and without, with two pretty little brass pieces (saluting guns) on carriages. Apart from pleasure, her other service is to send advice to Sir William's ships lying in the Downs or between London and Dover. Every month there is at least one ship either outward or homeward bound.

Being well provided with meat and drink, we dropped down the river one morning, Mr William Courteen, Capt. Molton, Mr Samuel Bunnell, myself and others, with the musick intended to go on board the ships. Setting sail from Billingsgate away she seemingly flew down the river of Thames, with a fair wind, colours displayed, shooting off our little guns, the Musick playing all the time, sometimes loud as Consorts of Cornets and Hautboys, sometimes soft as Vyolls so that, in my opinion it would have animated the dullest spirit to have forsaken all and followed the Sea.

At Woolwich we found the "Dragon", "Sun" and "Catherine" and having been entertained on board we all went ashore to see the great ship now building in Woolwich Dock under the supervision of Mr Pett. We were then shown the model of the ship which had been exhibited to His Majesty. It is of exquisite workmanship, painted and gilded with azure and gold, so contrived that every timber could be seen. The great ship itself will be ready for launching in April 1637 and she will be the greatest and fairest ever built in England. I think she is worthy to carry the Flag as Admiral of the Seas.

4th April 1636.   This day I went down in a ketch to carry goods and provisions to the ships in the Downs and in particular two trunks filled with plate and presents. I understand the plate, valued at £300 is allowed by our employers for the use of commanders and merchants: the presents are to be bestowed on Kings and governors of foreign countries as occasion requires.

A most unfortunate accident happened at this time. The "Anne Royal" being bound for the Downs, ran aground stern foremost on a bank on the Tilbury side in the night and as the tide dropped she began to fall over, most of the people on board being asleep. The Master, foreseeing danger tried to hurry his wife and daughter but they, being ashamed to be seen half dressed, delayed so long that the ship capsized and many perished. A boatswain's mate took his wife in his arms and leapt overboard but they were crushed between a boat and the ship's side. Here was modesty and love evily recompensed by the merciless sea.

CHAPTER IV

To India and the East Indies.
1635 to 1638.

Journal of a Voyage of a Fleet, consisting of four ships and two pinnaces set forth by Sir William Courteen for India, China, Japan etc. on a new discovery of traffic in those parts.

Our fleet consisted of the "Dragon", our admiral, Capt. John Weddell, the "Sun" Capt. Richard Swanley, the "Catherine" Capt. John Carter, the "Planter", Capt. Edward Hall, the "Anne" pinnace, Master Martin Milward and the "Discovery" pinnace, Master Richardson.

14th April 1636. Our whole fleet set sail from the Downs about three of the Clock in the afternoon.

17th April. (Easter Day) Our ships being then between Portland and the Start we hoisted our Colours and fired our ordnance.

30th April. We saw the Island of Lansarote (Canary Islands) high, mountainous and ragged land.

3rd May. In the morning we descried a fleet of 26 sail and coming nearer we made them out to be Spanish galleons bound for the West Indies.

We saw many Tortoises and with our skiff took three of them: very good meat.

18th May. We saw a great many shell fish or sea snails. Pricking one of them, it distilled some drops of a perfect azure: the head yielded purple. Whether this be the murex mentioned in the Histories, out of which they drew that precious purple, I know not. I wrote with it and it retained its colour.

23rd May. We had this day a violent gust. Our vice-admiral lost her main topmast and also a man who fell into the sea with the topmast and most of the rigging. The "Discovery" also lost her main topmast. Immediately all the carpenters in the fleet were sent aboard to make all good again which they did within the space of a week.

19th August. We saw a sail and our Admiral sent a barge to board her. She was a carrack from Lisbon bound for India and had on board 800 passengers including the Archbishop of India elect.

23rd August. We put into Johanna to refresh our men. The inhabitants are generally Moslems, poor black and unhandsome. There are some Arab merchants here that trade to Madagascar for ambergris, slaves etc. Herewith were a couple of junks, one of near 100 tons not yet finished, she being all sowed together.

27th September. A sett of fair weather, a gentle gale, a smooth sea.

6th October. At our approaching the Roads of Goa our Admiral sent the barge ashore with a letter to the Viceroy. The next day the galleons came out to meet us and we saluted each other with the firing of ordnance.

8th October. We anchored close to the castle of Agoada where we had the best peal of ordnance that I ever heard, all sides letting fly with a thundering noise and redoubling echo from the shore. Within a few days our King's letter was delivered to the Viceroy with a gold chain from which was suspended a portrait of our King and Queen.

23rd October. This day passed by four Hollanders we suppose bound for Swat. The Portuguese galleons chased them but could not overtake them.

27th October. Ten sail of Hollanders rode before the Port without permission of the authorities ashore.

11th January 1637. Before daybreak the Portuguese fleet of seven ships and 15 or 16 frigates approached the Hollanders who were surprised and began to throw lumber overboard to clear their decks. The fight began at six in the morning and lasted until noon when the Portuguese retired into the harbour. One of the latter lost her main topmast and was in danger of sinking but our English carpenters helped to plug the holes. What I write about this fight is by relation as I was in the city at the time. This month ran away from us three of our tallest men. They are concealed by the Portuguese who now stand in need of such men especially gunners.

The island of Goa is somewhat hilly with valleys very fruitful by Nature and art, having many fountains and springs. The city is some four or five miles around with some fair streets, fair buildings

and many goodly churches. Monasteries and colleges are as fair to
see without as rich and beautifully adorned within.

The Monastery of the Carmelites was fired by accident whilst
we were there but nobody hurt. At the Jesuits house our
commanders and merchants were feasted by the padres and after
dinner entertained with good choral music accompanied with the
harp and Spanish gitterne: our English music was also there. The
house is situated in a most delicious shady grove on the side of a
hill, with tall and flourishing fruit trees, pleasant springs and
walks.

In this garden I first saw the pepper plant growing up at the foot
of the areca or betel nut tree: this part of the country affords no
pepper for merchanise, only the plant in some gardens as a rarity.
Cocotrees have only one stem with a great bush at the top. It
affords meat, drink and lodging; oil, milk, sugar etc. and good
cordage is made of the outward rind.

At our being here a new galleon of 140 feet by the keel was
launched, being first blessed, christened and named by the
Archbishop as El buen Jesus. She was launched in a device wherein
she was built, called a cradle. I went aboard her. She is said to be of
1600 tons, of a strange form: twelve main shrouds aside; steered
below with tackles fastened to her tiller: all monstrous methought.

A Jesuit showed us at the College of Bon Jesus a monument or
tomb of Francisco Xavier, the great reputed saint. It is of silver of
good workmanship with several stories of his life embossed. On
his Holy Day there is much good music and at night pretty
fireworks, their church and steeple set with multitude of lights.
There are many festivals in the year whereon they bestow great
cost in pageants and shows. Thus they spend part of their idle
time.

In imitation of Spanish bullbaiting they ran a couple of buffa-
loes, one after the other. The first unhorsed an hidalgo and the
second killed a negro. The Viceroy has a couple of elephants which
are put to work to draw timber.

By history and report the Portuguese had a flourishing time in
these parts being absolute masters and commanders in these seas.
Then they bestowed their wealth in building churches, fair dwelling houses in city and country with rich furniture and fine gardens;
spending their time in pleasure, ease and recreation. But those days

are past, much abated by the coming of the English and Dutch.

17th January.   In the morning we set sail from Goa exchanging farewell guns with the fort and galleons and stood to the southward. The Dutch presently weighed (anchor) and came with us.

18th January.   We parted with the Hollanders.

23rd January.   We anchored under a small island to the northward of Battacala. There lay here about 200 vessels, among them 16 bigger vessels with topmasts, being the Cinnamon fleet come from Ceylon, some frigates of war for convoy, the rest with rice and provisions, all bound for Goa.

23rd February.   In the afternoon we came to some Pepper gardens which they manure and dress and then set out ranks of tall young betel nut trees. At the base of these are planted the pepper plants which climb up the former like the ivy does the oak. They continue ten or twelve years yielding good pepper. The crop is dried in the sun. The kernel of the berry is the pepper itself.

28th February.   The King invited us to supper, where our table cloth and dishes were of plantain leaves sewn together. We had at least twenty sorts of pickled fruit as mangoes, cardomons green peppers etc to relish meats. In our dishes we had milk, sweet and sour, and syrups of several sorts. Rice we had dressed in sundry manners. The King sat by us with a rod, pointing to this or that he would have us eat. After supper he gave us permission to build a house (factory) at Battacola and to trade in his country.

At our arrival at Bhatkal we understood that pestilential fevers had swept through the fleet. We have lost out of our little ship "Planter" most of our principal officers. In all the fleet we have lost fourscore, the sickness yet continuing. God in his mercy assuage it.

27th March.   We came to Cochin, anchored there and saluted the town with our ordnance. Cochin is a very large town with many churches and monasteries but not so fair as at Goa. Few Portuguese of quality – mostly half-castes. Here we bought a parcel of cinnamon to help make up the "Planter's" cargo. There were sent aboard some bullocks and hogs free.

31st March.   We weighed from Cochin and proceeded on our voyage.

4th April.   We came to Cape Comorin.

6th April.   The "Planter" took leave of us and sailed for

England. Her lading was mostly pepper, with cinnamon, frankincense and gum lac.

7th April. We passed the fair island of Ceylon where groweth the best cinnamon in the world. This morning we saw a very high hill resembling somewhat the crown of our now new fashion hats.

19th April. We were in sight of the Island of Sumatra. Achin lies at the north end of Sumatra and is thought to be that Ophir from which King Solomon had his gold, apes and peacocks. At our anchoring came boats aboard from the King bearing his Choppe or Seal, a token of favour and safeconduct. The principal officers and merchants of the fleet were invited to witness a great ceremoney. The great green was decorated with flags. First came a squadron of elephants with little low turrets on their backs, and in each a soldier in red with a lance, standing upright. The first rank of elephants had long iron scythes fastened to their tusks. Next came a number of elephants with turrets whereon were placed small guns each with a man to manage them. The next rank had bows and arrows, darts etc. Then cometh the King on a great and stately elephant richly adorned and covered down to the feet. At his issuing forth the music played as Hautboys, trumpets and drums. All the aforesaid music discordant, clamourous and full of noise.

The houses at Achin are built on posts covered with palm leaves, the sides of rattans very prettily woven. The living is in the upper rooms, the lower lying open like a linhay. After some great showers of rain, the valley is overflown and they go from house to house in prahus or boats.

2nd May. We set sail from Achin at break of day.

11th May. We came to a small island called Pulovera which was by our commander renamed Hope Island, taking possession of it for the King of England by nailing a leaden plate with the English arms on a tree. Here we wooded and watered.

15th and 16th May. We saw the mainland of Malacca and the island of Sumatra.

24th May. We anchored in the road of Malacca and saluted the town. It is very strong, being furnished with near 160 pieces of brass ordnance. The Master Gunner is an Englishman long since run away from one of the Company's ships and married to a Portuguese half-caste.

Here is also an Englishwoman married to a Portuguese half-caste of some quality, having between them one pretty boy. She came from England 18 or 19 years ago in the "Unicorn", being maid servant to one Furbisher, a carpenter, and his family. After some adventures she was befriended by the Portuguese and married to this man who has a post in the Custom House. Her name was Judith and is now Julia de la gracia.

This part of the Continent is properly called Malaya and the Malay tongue is used far and near.

27th June.   We passed in among islands and came to anchor three leagues distance from Macao. We saluted the place with our ordnance but a boat came out warning us not to proceed until we had permission from the Governor of the city. Macao is at one end of an island and is built on rising hills. The houses are double tiled and even then plastered over for security against hurricanes.

29th June.   The City sent us a present of refreshing viz. eight beeves, eight hogs, eight jars of sweetmeats, eight bags of bread and some fruit.

1st July.   There came a China Mandarin aboard with other Chinese to know what we intended so that they could inform their master who is a great Mandarin at Canton. He was apparelled in a gown of black sarsanette or tiffany and under that other garments, with strange attire on his head. He had carried before him a large board written in Chinese characters; it seemed to be the badge of his authority.

12th July.   Came five long large lighter-like vessels laden with goods from Canton where the Portuguese make yearly invest-ments. In the past two days we careened the ships to make them clean and to kill the (teredo) worm that consumes them in these parts.

22nd July.   We had a rumour that the "Anne" had been seized but this proved false and that evening she returned, finding great encouragement of trade from the Chineses. But the Portuguese would report us to be pirates and that we only came to rob and spoil. In conclusion, finding but bad hopes from the Portuguese of any good to be done in matter of trade, yet encouragement from the Chinese we determined to leave this place.

29th July 1637.   We came forth from Macao. Before we left the Churchmen sent us good ripe grapes, figs and pears.

August 1637.   That night we weighed and came northward into the bay towards the mouth of the river of Canton. During the last two days we saw a great number of fishing boats and other craft and it may be verified that in China there are more people on the water than on the land.

4th August. During the past four days we have got little farther owing to strong currents and slight winds. Another fleet of great Chinese junks including the King's men-of-war numbering 40 strange vessels, strangely fitted. They desired us to anchor which we did and kept especially good watch that night, not knowing as yet how to trust them.

6th August. Came a messenger with an interpreter from the Mandarin of the fleet desiring us to proceed no farther towards Canton but to turn aside to a place called Lantau where we should have provisions and that they would also endeavour we should have admittance of trade.

8th August. We came to a convenient place and anchored in ten or eleven fathoms of water. On the starboard side on land, a platform was being erected which was supplied with men and ordnance, making preparations for enemies whilst we meant them no harm.

9th August. We sent ashore to the Fort and receiving some bad answer to our peaceable demands we fitted ourselves for offence as well as defence, displaying our bloody ensigns on our poops, putting on our waistbands and the King's colours on our maintops which the Chinois perceiving sent a messenger desiring us to have patience for six more days. With this we were pacified for the time.

We went to a Pagoda of theirs, a reasonable handsome building and well tiled. On the altar was an image of a woman, having on her head an ornament resembling an Imperial crown. A little distance away were two images of Mandarins with fans in their hands and two evil favoured, fiend-like figures. Before the altar there burned a lamp and great standing cups, 4 or 5 feet high, whereon they burn incense with many small candles sticking in sundry places. There hung a bell within the said pagoda of about 4 or 5 cwt of cast iron or some alloy which they strike with a wooden club.

The people there gave us a certain drink called Chaa which is only water with a kind of herb boiled in it. It must be drank warm and is accounted wholesome. (Char or tea).

15th August.   Came a petty Mandarin with a flag of truce to know our grievances: he promised to do his best that we might have our desires for free trade, a place for our ships and a house on shore. The next day came the same Mandarin and desired that two persons should be appointed to go with him to Canton to put in our petition. So Mr John Mountney and Mr Thomas Robinson went with the Mandarin in his own junk and they carried for presents a richly ornamented cabinet, a basin and ewer of silver etc. So now there appeared some hopes of setting up a trade in these parts.

21st August.   Our Mandarin came again bringing a patent in Chinese writing, pasted on a great board, granting us leave to buy and sell any commodity in their country and appointing three anchorages for our ships. The Mandarin desired that two of our merchants should go to Canton to look over such items as gold, musk, raw silk and other materials. As for sugar, porcelain, green ginger, china roots etc. these could be obtained locally. That night we restored all the guns we had taken from the platform or fort.

1st September.   Came a letter from our merchants at Canton desiring us to return again down river to our old anchorage advising also that they had already bought 2,000 sugar loaves and were sending them down the next day. Notwithstanding this advice we decided to remain where we were.

5th September.   Came Mr Robinson and the Mandarin from Canton and next day much sugar for loading and provisions for the ships, including pears, chestnuts and dried lychees as sweet as any raisins of the sun.

Came from Macao three junks with many Portuguese bringing a protest from the authorities there and declaring that unless we left the coast they would complain to both our Kings and require satisfaction but we forthwith answered this protest in a slighting answer and they departed.

Sunday 10th September.   It pleased God to deliver us from a treacherous and dangerous plot to have us destroyed by fire. About two in the morning, the ships being lately careened went down with the ebb tide: The little Anne in the lead espied several great junks under sail approaching but let them pass thinking they might have goods to put aboard our fleet. Two of the junks were now alight and in flames. The "Catherine" gave a warning and our ships cut their cables and made sail to avoid the danger. One of the junks went ashore, two were carried up river and out of sight and another was fired accidentally. The fire was very high and violent and the brightness so great in that dark night that the hills reflected light. All this lasted about two hours. By that time the junks were consumed and we, by God's providence freed from that great danger and quieted.

By Francisco, a Portuguese slave who had escaped from his owners and from the Chinese, we heard that there were 15 Portuguese at Canton negotiating against us, that a fleet of fire junks was being prepared. He also warned us that we should not eat or drink any provisions sent from the shore as it would be poisoned.

27th September. We came within four leagues of Macao and there anchored. Came a boat from Macao with a Jesuit and a Spaniard, a Serjauntt Major who came aboard the "Sun". Necessity compelling us, we sent a letter to Macao desiring in friendly manner that they would procure the release of our merchants (at Canton).

4th October. At noon Mr Woolman and myself were sent to the Bay to see whether it would be better anchorage for our ships. Whilst there we were invited on board the great galleon of Manilla, being kindly entertained and lodged that night. The galleon was about 700 tons, very strong in timber work and stout sided. She had made one voyage to Acapulco and back. From Manilla she brought 9 or 10 tons of Cloves, dye wood and tobacco. Our seamen who also stayed the night on board said that even the inferior officers, such as Boatswains, Carpenters etc. used some silver plates. In the great Cabin there was certainly a variety. It seems they make rich voyages from Manilla to Nova Hispanna and back again. Aboard this ship was the first time I tasted Chacculatte (chocolate), although I had heard it spoken of. It is made of a certain grain growing in the West Indies. These they dry, grind to powder, boil in water, add sugar, spice, odours etc; drinking it warm in the mornings is accounted very wholesome.

At last we had permission from the Portuguese for a limited trade in Macao so we hired a house and settled some of our people ashore, selling cloth, incense etc and buying sugar, green ginger and some materials whilst waiting for our merchants to be released from Canton. At last we heard that they were come to within a league of the town but it proved false. However on the 10th November we had a letter from them that they had freighted two great junks with sugar, green ginger, sugar candy and china roots and hoped to come down themselves very soon.

12th November. Before the lodgings of the Captain of the Manilla galleon, a scaffold or theatre was erected whereon was acted a play by Chinese boys. The boys were well favoured and their singing somewhat like that in India, all in unison, keeping in time with tabours and copper vessels. It was done in the open place to all comers without money being demanded. We were also invited to see a play acted in St. Paul's Church by the children of the town. It was to depict the life of their much renowned Saint Francisco Xavier. The children were very pretty and richly adorned in apparel and precious jewels, it being the parents care to set them forth for their own content and credit, as it was the Jesuits to instruct them, who not only in this but in all other manner of education are tutors and have the care of bringing up the youth and young children of this town.

28th November. Our long expected merchants arrived.

A Chinaman eating with chopsticks. One of Mundy's own sketches.

CHAPTER V

Voyage Home from Macao

1638

30th Dec. 1637. We passed the Galleon of Manilla. We gave her five guns and she answered with eleven. Calm and the weather warm.

3rd Jan. 1638. One Hubert, a Dutchman, a proper lusty fellow, fell out of the "Sun's" maintop into the sea, so they flung a buoy overboard to him and left him to try for his life for a while. The "Sun" hath been unfortunate, for out of her crew of 132, she has lost 52 dead from sickness, 4 drowned, one killed and 9 run away: in all 66.

4th Jan. Thick and misty. Last night goodman Anthony, in our ship the "Dragon" going to heave the log, fell overboard and crying "O Lord! O Lord" was no more heard of, it being night, the ship with very fresh way. Some said he could not swim at all.

12th Jan. This day we met with three Dutch vessels who told us the news from Europe: the East India ship "Palsgrave" had been cast ashore and Sir William Courteen had died. They also desired us to hand over any Portuguese, together with their goods, to them but we denied that we had any. Some hours passed in debate but at length our admiral produced his Commission from his Majesty giving him power to make reprisals and they did not further molest us.

16th Jan. We came to anchor in Malacca Road.

13th February. The "Dragon" set sail for India leaving us to take in what goods could be procured and depart for England in the "Sun".

28th Feb. Mr Edward Knipe having business with the King of Achin, Capt. Swanly and myself went with him. At the entrance to the Court gate, we put off our shoes and coming near the King made obeissance by joining our hands palm to palm and lifted them over our heads. Then we sat down crosslegged to behold the sport of Cockfighting. The King was very familiar, of a settled countenance although hard favoured and adorned with many jewels and diamonds. Having our demands granted we all three got up on our elephant. I was badly seated and found it very uneasy riding – the beast had such a shuffling, jogging and justling pace. At last we alighted from its back to the upper gallery of our house which saved the labour of going upstairs.

At our arrival here we found an Englishman in a small vessel trading for himself. His name was Dig(ory) Penkeu of St Minver and he was born in the Westcountry and was friendly and courteously entertained by us. But he secretly left in his vessel, having got into debt and making away with some of our money. But it pleased God that within a day or two he was driven by foul weather on shore, his goods spoiled, having his crew run away and himself left to repent.

Saturday 3rd March.   About two o'clock in the morning we set sail from Achin, having taken in about 37 tons of pepper, bending our course homewards.

13th April.   We had sight of the Island of Mauritius and put in there principally to look for a leak, also to water and refresh our men. We met no dodos, yet divers times they are found here,

The Dodo

having seen two at Surat brought from hence; as I remember they are as big as large turkies, covered with down, having little hanging wings like short sleeves altogether useless to fly with or to help themselves. They cannot swim properly and being cloven footed behave in the water like other land birds.

Our captain left a letter on Cooper's Island adjoining the harbour giving details of our voyage and stay here: it was put into a hole made with an auger in a piece of wood and hung up in a tree for the next comet. We expected to have found some letters here but we found none. Letters are usually placed in stone bottles which are sealed and hung bottom upwards.

18th April.   About noon we set sail from Mauritius.

2nd May.   We cut up the great boat that we bought at Achin because the heavy seas were smashing it against the ship's side and causing damage. Water had seeped down between the decks and spoiled some silks of mine because I had trusted too much to others.

Having taken in so much water by seas and leaks that our men had much ado to free her with two chain pumps and baling we felt it would be impossible to weather the Cape of Good Hope and decided to put into Madagascar. So we bore up before the wind when by and bye another sea came astern and broke into the great Cabin although the ports had been made fast with bars and boards.

9th June.   We went with our skiff to the New River which was much altered since my last being here nearly ten years ago. Returning homewards we had sight of the biggest alligator or crocodile I ever saw.

10th June.   Mr Thomas Woolman, our Master, died and was buried in a decent manner with three vollies of small shot and four pieces of great ordnance. A store of lemons was brought aboard.

2nd August.   It pleased God to send us in to our comfort the ship "Planter" who did willingly supply us. Our cargo was then removed to the sternmost part of the ship so that the carpenters and officers of both vessels could inspect the foreparts for leaks. We were asked whether we would go back to India but one and all replied in a joint voice that we would rather hazard going home in a leaky ship to our Native Country.

28th August.   We set sail from Madagascar.

25th September.   We had sight of the Cape of Good Hope.

8th October. We had sight of the island of St Helena, our Captain having decided to proceed directly there instead of putting in at the Cape, since all our men were in good health, with fresh water enough and a fair wind.

9th October. We anchored between Lemon and Chapel valleys. Going on shore we found the Chapel newly repaired by the Dutch. The names of divers ships, principal men and some women were fairly written on boards fixed within the Chapel.

13th October. At night we set sail from St Helena.

25th October. For the past month it hath pleased God to lend us such fair weather, smooth seas and favourable winds that we had scarce our tacks aboard nor lowered our topgallant sails.

13th November. We mounted our ordnance and prepared our ship, as we were drawing near to where we might equally meet with foes as with friends.

12th December. We passed very near the Isles of Scilly.

15th December. We came to Dover road. That evening we took post horses and rode all night.

16th December. Early in the morning we came to London. Our company in very good health. God's name be praised.

Among our company were two old men not to be forgotten. The one Antonio Gonsalez, a Portugal who was taken by Sir Francis Drake, was with him in the West Indies when he died, married an Englishwoman, and now homeward bound, grew blind, a good, honest, poor old Man. The other was Father Avery, our Cook, who came aboard at Gravesend, and although we touched at sundry parts, the ship lying near the shore, boats and skiffs continually going to and from the ships, yet was he not known to set his foot on land (although in good health) until the ship arrived at Erith, being carried ashore there to be buried, having died as the ship came up the River.

A rail – Ascension Island (now extinct). One of Peter Mundy's own sketches.

CHAPTER VI

A Petty Progresse through Some Parts of England and Wales

1639

19th June 1639. The following journey I undertook partly to follow my disposition to travel and partly (to free myself of some inconveniences I found by living at home in the country) to seek some other residence. Every day's journey is not set down but only places and notable happenings which occurred, directing my course first towards Bristol. On the day aforesaid I departed from Penryn in Cornwall. The next day I came to Stratton, an ancient town noted for the best garlic. A little beyond this place I crossed the Tamar which divides Cornwall from Devon and has its source but a few miles from the Bristol Channel, wanting but little to make Cornwall an island.

I passed through Bideford where is a stone bridge of about 25 arches over a creek, the largest I have yet seen in England; there be small vessels belonging to this place.

I next lay at Barnstaple, a large and neat town and a sea port, many vessels belonging to it. At morning prayer in the church on a week day, 30 vessels were named as being absent in sundry voyages. There is a pretty exchange with a large stone before it like a tomb. It serves now, as I was told, to pay or tender money thereon, also to seal writings, covenants etc and goes by the name of Barnstaple stone.

In fine a handsome and well governed town with much trade Tiverton, twice burned by accident (1598 and 1612). A capacious church and the greatest audience at one sermon that I ever saw. I was told that within these last three or four days there fell so much snow that it lay two or three feet deep so that many sheep perished; strange at this time of the year.

Glastonbury. Here were the ruins of a famous abbey, most part down, the rest daily decaying. Among the ruins as they now dig for stones for other buildings are many tombs. The kitchen is yet

51

entire and made entirely of hewn stone: it now serves to store turf for fuel. Near this place is a thorn tree that flourisheth about mid winter but it now stands neglected by the highway, ready to fall down with age. There are others about the town, probably cuttings from the same tree. It is by the country people termed the Holy Thorn.

Wells.   This hath a very fair cathedral church and an excellent dial showing not only the hours and quarters but every minute. The age of the moon also.

Bath.   From whence I came to Bath, a pretty little city and a fine market house. But of all England's wonders the King's Bath deserves the first place. The heat is as much as a man may suffer at the springs. I saw Men and Women go in together and those that will may have guides. No incivility permitted, under pain of punishment. The Earl of Northumberland was here at this time in the Bath and his guide, to make him sport, lay upon the water on his back, with both hands under his head. This place much frequented by gentry, especially at the spring and fall of the leaf.

27th June.   I came to the city of Bristol. The city very clean and dry by reason they say most of the houses have vaulted sinks which convey the water and filth into the river. They also use sleds and not carts. Here at Ratcliffe is a great church, not quite finished, built at the charge of Mr Canynge, a citizen and great shipowner. By the High Cross is the exchange where are many curious, costly pillars of brass, about 3 to 4 feet high for men to lean on and pay money. A pretty bridge with a little street on it like that at London. In conclusion Bristol is even a little London for merchants, shipping and great and well furnished markets and I think second to it in the kingdom of England. Here is a general custom to serve beer in large silver beakers in all inns and taphouses. Also scarce a house that hath not a dog to turn the spit in a little wooden wheel. I was almost tempted by the commodiousness plenty and pleasantness of the place to have taken up my habitation here, but I had a mind to see farther first.

16th July.   I came to the city of Gloucester. It is a reasonable handsome quiet and cleanly place: no great trafficking for land and sea. In the church is the tomb of William Courthose, brother to William Rufus, his image made of Irish oak, firm and solid, it being about 540 years since he died.

Being now at Gloucester and Wales so near I had a desire to see some of that country also and first came to Rosse, then to Abergavenny where one Rice Morgan or Rice the Cantor, a Welsh harper, with his excellent playing on that instrument and my own plying Welsh ale, I was at length so charmed that almost all my money with divers things were gone out of my pocket. And riding from thence about a mile from the town, my horse threw me into a deep, dirty pool of water, over head and ears. At length I got up, some bruised and came to Langtwyne, a village where I was fain to pawn a little money to carry me back to Gloucester to fetch more to redeem my sword again.

Next morning I came to Brecknock where I heard service in Welsh. From here I took my journey towards Hereford. There is a great Cathedral church and good voices, especially the boys when they sang together with the rest of the choir.

1st August 1639. I set out from Gloucester towards Worcester. That night I lay at Tewkesbury: the mustard of this place is much spoken of.

2nd August. I came to the city of Worcester. Fair and well paved streets, high in the middle with kennels on both sides. Many clothiers. A fair Cathedral church with the fairest pair of organs that I have yet seen. Before the altar lyeth the monument of King John. And prince Arthur, Henry the 7th's eldest son lyeth in a pretty chapel, although a plain tomb. Here is a water-house (reservoir) which serveth the city, most houses having pipes: others have it brought them in leather bags on horses. In conclusion it is a very delightsome city, the River Severn adjacent, on whose banks as I came were many anglers, generally very smart and elegant in their tackle such as rods of cane with fine tops etc.

3rd August. I returned towards Gloucester by Malvern hills. In the river Severn about Gloucester at new and full moon there is a sudden, swift and violent rushing forward of the flood tide against the current from the river. The water rises till at length the sea overmasters the river and driveth it back before him.

7th August. I departed from Gloucester and about 20 miles in our way came to Burford. Between these two places we passed over some of the Cotswold Downs, of which the wool is much celebrated. From Burford we came to Eynsham ferry where we crossed the river Isis and from thence to Oxford.

Oxford. Things notable are the many stately, spacious and commodious colleges, founded by kings, queens and famous persons. Also the great number of pretty, civil, well featured and nurtured youth, their long gowns and four cornered caps becoming them better, in my opinion, than any other habit. In the chapel of Magdalene College is a pretty marble monument of two brethren named Thomas and John Littleton who going to recreate themselves in the Thames, one of them fell in: the other going to help his brother they were suddenly and unhappily both drowned. Christchurch, also very excellently set forth with fair windows of scriptures in lively coloured painted glass set up but last year (1638). The said church was built by Cardinal Wolsey. The city has one extraordinary long, fair street (the High) going down to Magdalene College: a great many booksellers and two printers belonging to the University.

16th August. I came to London, passing through several towns, Abingdon, where is a pretty cross, Henley-upon-Thames, Maidenhead, Colnbrook, Brentford etc.

10th September. I took my journey to see Stourbridge Fair, so much celebrated and accounted the biggest held in England. At Theobald they showed me the chamber where King James died and King Charles his bedstead, boarded as in Spain: he is said to sleep also on quilted beds in the summer time as they do there. Here is a fair garden with spacious walks. At St Albans is the supposed tomb of Sir John Mandeville, the traveller, of whom a book bears the name, supposed never to be made by him, there being so many incredulous stories and unlikelihoods.

11th September. I took my way towards Cambridge and passed by Royston where is another of the King's houses. There being nobody at home, I could not get in. This is a wonderful corn country as might be judged by the tillage, and plenty of good ale and beer here to be had.

Cambridge on the outside hath nothing near the fair prospect Oxford hath. That evening I lay in Trinity College, being invited by some students, not of the highest rank. What entertainment I had of them and what other passages happened between us will be too prolix for this place.

12th September. I went down the river Granta in a tilted boat (i.e. one with an awning for shelter) and came to the place where

Stourbridge Fair is kept in a field with tents and booths set out in streets and lanes bearing their particular names, plentifully furnished with all manner of commodities, especially hops of which I think there were not less than 2,000 bags lying in the fields: also wool, cloth, salt fish, tar, plate, brass ware, wooden ware even old boots and shoes, and near 40 wine taverns. So having tasted some of their wine and good Lynn beer out of boats that came from hence, and eaten some of their oysters I left the Fair and came back to Cambridge that evening by land. I had forgot the multitude of alehouses, victualling houses etc. Next morning I walked the streets and saw the Colleges, King's College Chapel is a lofty stately building and much beautifies the place. It hath very high and rich windows of scripture stories in coloured glass.

13th September. I came from Cambridge and so to Ware where I was shewn the great bed. I conceive the bedstead to be between 9 and 10 feet square, wherein may lie 8 persons.

14th September. I came again to London, never wanting company on that great road especially at fair time.

26th September. I took my journey towards the Downs to see the fleet riding there and came to Rochester. From thence to Chatham where five ships of the Navy were ready to go down to the Downs. A mile below is Gillingham before which rode the great Royal Sovereign which I saw on the stocks in April 1636 when we embarked on our China voyage. Her head, waist, quarter and stern so enriched with carved work overlaid with gold that it appears most glorious even from afar, especially her spacious lofty stern. Her inside is admirably contrived: neat spacious cabins, steered by tackles on the tiller, directed from aloft by a speaking tube wherein the voice is conveyed to them below: her cookroom in the hold, the work therein being done by candlelight. She is said to carry 92 brass pieces of ordnance. She hath five great lanterns: in the biggest may stand 12 or 13 men. By Chatham is the King's Yard wherein are two docks. Near the yard the Ropemaker's Field, wherein is the longest roof that ever I saw (excepting the long gallery at Paris). This serves in time of rain for the ropemakers to spin their yarn. There was no lodging to be had in Chatham by reason of the number of seamen arriving to man the King's ships.

27th September. Taking my journey towards Deal I passed through Canterbury in whose Cathedral is the richest and neatest

Battle of the Downs between

font that ever I saw, of marble both white and black, with a fair gilt iron rail round the cover. Being now come to Deal, I saw from the beach, a great fleet extending for nearly three miles and numbering about 160 ships. 52 were Spanish, about 80 or 90 Hollanders and the rest English, all seeming to be one fleet. Such a warlike fleet was never known in our age to be together. The Hollanders have sundry vessels riding to seaward to watch that no more Spaniards escape to Dunkirk. I went aboard the Spanish admiral called the "Santiago", about 1,000 tons burthen with 800 men and 60 guns. From thence I went aboard the "Santa Teresa", galleon of Portugal the fairest and biggest ship of them all, about 1,100 tons. She was

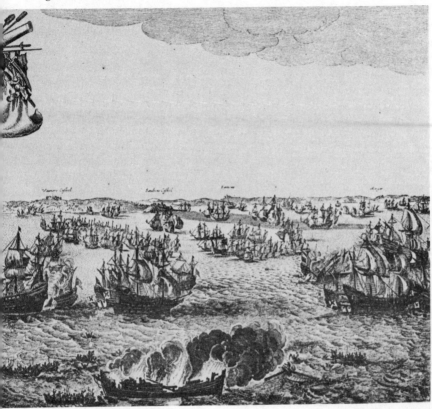

Dutch and Spanish Fleets, 1639

built as an East India carrack. The Spaniards have abundance of
men but most part sickly, tattered and inexpert as souldiers or
sailors: all in general perplexed but preparing for the fight again
and repairing what hath been damaged by the Hollanders in the
late skirmish. They have now a sickness amongst them and many
die, whose bodies being flung overboard, some of them are washed
ashore along the beach. Both Hollander and Spaniard come ashore
to buy provisions in the market, one among the other as friends.

Then went I aboard the English admiral, Sir John Pennington in
the "Unicorn" and from thence aboard the Dutch admiral in the
"Amelia", where I found the Hollanders lusty, healthy and

frolicksome, encouraged by former success and this present for-
tunate opportunity. They have in their fleet 8 or 10 fireships fitted
with chains, grapnells etc.

1st October. I came to London again, meeting many lords,
knights and gentry posting to and fro, some about business but
most to see news, as did multitudes of the common sort.

14th October. Upon the rumour of the fight having begun
between the Hollander and the Spaniard, I returned to the Downs
in company of another friend but before our arrival all was over.
There we saw some of the ruined Spanish fleet, seven vessels
ashore, one burned and the others utterly lost. The local people
were at work at some wrecks, breaking them up for the timber and
iron. About 14 other ships were at anchor but with little hope of
getting clear. The Dutch fleet now returned from the fight was
riding within a league of Deal. Many hundreds of the poor
Spaniards were in Deal and the neighbouring country begging. By
the colour of their clothes they seemed to be labourers and other
poor people and confessed that they were betrayed in their own
country, being surprised by officers, taken bound, sent to prison
and from thence aboard ships.

The beginning of the fight, by relation of credible eye-witnesses,
was on Friday morning early at which time all the Hollanders were
under sail and making towards the Spaniards. The King's ships also
set sail. The Dutch fired as they drew near the Spanish vessels and
were then themselves fired upon by the King's ships as forbidding
them to offer violence in the King's chamber to his friends. But
that would not avail. The Hollanders ignored the English fire but
pressed on towards the Spaniards and sent fire ships among them.
Twenty two or three Spaniards immediately ran ashore on the
beach and two or three were fired. The rest made to sea and the
Hollander after. From Deal we returned to London again.

Matters of note which I saw at London are:
first our King's Majesty playing at Pell Mell by St James and the
Queen's Majesty at mass in Whitehall, the Queen, Prince Charles
and the Duke of York in Cheapside at my Lord Mayor's show
who was then Sir Henry Garraway who was one of the committee
for the East India Company when I first went to India in 1628.

The "Sovereign of the Seas"

CHAPTER VII

Travels to Holland and around the Baltic

1639–1647

A Passage from England over into Holland with some particulars of that Country.

16th March 1639.   Being bound for Holland, I determined to take my passage in a small ketch with a few other passengers but finding a larger ship, the "Content" due to sail two days later, I determined to wait.

20th March.   I came to Gravesend having got a pass from the Custom House. The "Content" arrived the same night and I was told that the ketch was probably already arrived in Holland, having had extraordinary fair weather and a good wind. Our ship was due to meet another vessel on which my Lord Craven was to take passage so we stayed all the next day, a Saturday, as well as the following.

23rd March.   We set sail from Gravesend having taken aboard three horses for the Queen of Bohemia and certain English soldiers passing over to serve the States.

24th March.   Although the wind would well have served us, the other ship put into Queenborough (I conceive for his Lordship's ease or health) and we followed. Since my coming to Gravesend the winds have been variable and contrary, much frost and snowing hard. From hence (Queenborough) and Feversham are great store of great Kentish oysters transported to London and the Low Countries.

28th March.   We set to sea but before morning the wind came contrary with such vehemency that it grew to a storm so that we returned, hoping to put into Queenborough. But our mainsail was not set, being so heavy that it was thought likely to carry away the mast and in any case the men could not handle so. So we were forced to drop anchor, whilst we watched our consort pass by us

and put into Queenborough. We had not rode long before the
cable broke. We let go another anchor and the keel struck on the
sands in a violent manner and we expected the vessel to have split
in sunder and sunk. Then had there been but little hope of saving
our lives, it being nearly 1½ miles to the shore and extremely foul,
cold weather. No small boat was able to brook it, nor would ours
have been capable of taking a quarter of our company of 60
persons. But it pleased God to deliver us out of this danger by the
flood tide. Near upon full sea we set sail, steering towards the
shore and the ship nearly grounding on several occasions. The
master wrung his hands for if she struck with the water now
ebbing, there had been little hope of us. At last we put back into
Feversham.

4th April.   We set forth from Feversham and with the help of a
pilot came to the North Foreland.

5th April.   In the afternoon we put over for the coast of
Holland and sailed all that night with a fair wind. Next morning by
sounding we found ourselves in shoal water with a depth of five to
seven fathoms, as we thought on the banks off Flanders. The
morning proving so dusky, hazy and misty so that we could not
discern far from us, we put to seaward again, and then in again and
repeated this sundry times, all the time fearing we might be
surprised and pillaged by Dunkirkers. We then saw two sail make
towards us who proved to be English come over to take away
plaice and other fish. They told us where we were and that the
steeple which we now saw was Westkapelle on the island of
Walcheren.

7th April.   In the morning the wind increased so that once
again we felt ourselves in as bad a case as ever, fearing to be driven
off the coast by violence. But God also sent a remedy to this for a
pilot came aboard us and brought us into Brill.

7th April.   That night there was so much wind that the house
wherein we were, trembled and shook as with an earthquake.

A Cavat at warning.

I have the more detailed this passage for two reasons. The first that
had I kept my first resolution, I had avoided all the dangers and
troubles, besides expense and ill accommodation, the ship being
full of soldiers and encumbered with woolsacks: the second is that

I have undergone in these 15 days five times more hazards in coming but 45 leagues, than I have done these 25 years in sailing above 25,000 leagues. These are the chances of the world.

8th April.   I departed from the Brill towards Rotterdam.

Rotterdam is a place of much shipping and trade. Many English dwellers here and dress as at home. Here on the Groote Markt stands the statue of Erasmus, well cast in bronze.

10th April.   I went in a schuit or boat to the Hague, which boats go daily every hour from Rotterdam to Delft for three stivers. At Delft we landed and passing through the town, took boat again. From hence to the Hague they leave every half hour, the fare being 2 stivers. These boats set away precisely at the sound of a little bell, whether they have freight or not, drawn by one horse which goest at a good round trot about three miles an hour. Very cheap travelling and easy through the canals which are cast up by hand and filled by the water drawn from lower ground by windmills, whereof there are very many.

Delft is a fine and very clean town, the prettiest piazza I have yet seen, the fair Townhouse at one end and at the other the church, with a lofty steeple. In the church is a very costly monument, of marble and brass, to William the Silent, prince of Orange.

The Hague is the place where the Prince keeps his Court. Many stately edifices. From the Hague I returned to Rotterdam.

13th April.   I took passage for Amsterdam by boat. In all the way not a town of any quality, the ground all low and marshy.

Haarlem.   Within a few days I went to Haarlem about which is some rising ground, many pretty groves and woods. A little beyond the town are certain dunes where breed rabbits, of which many are brought to Amsterdam. Rivers and fountains of good water are very scarce in this part of the country and in Amsterdam their best water is what they save from the rain.

At Amsterdam, when building a house, they must drive in certain timbers 42 or 43 feet before they meet with any solid foundation: these timbers are said to last hundreds of years as long as they lie in moist earth. They are forced in by a certain engine, being a great weight. The weight, with the help of a large pulley is forced up and falling, driveth the piles into the sand.

Everyone goes to what church he pleases. A toleration here of all sects of religion.

The Stadthouse at Amsterdam

The Westerkirk, now building is the neatest of the churches: the steeple 300 feet high and in it a bell weighing 16,000 lbs. From the top of the tower is a fair view of Leyden and Utrecht in the distance and near at hand as fair and delightsome as I ever saw for a city. Most of the chief streets and canals as the Singelgracht, Heerengracht, Prinzengracht and Keisersgracht, alongside which many of the great merchants dwell, with pretty gardens. The canals and streets so long, so straight: the buildings so fair and uniform: ranks of trees on each side of the canal before their doors as in Moorfields in London so that they seem pleasant walks rather than city streets.

The Jews mostly came from Portugal and many are rich merchants, not evil esteemed of, living in liberty, wealth and ease; the men swarthy and thereby known from others but not by their habit. They allow pictures in their houses (not so at Constantinople), yea, some of them are painters.

As for the art of painting and the liking of the people for pictures, I think they are unsurpassed. There have been many eminent painters and some here at present, including Rembrandt. They strive to adorn their houses especially the outer or street room, with costly pieces. Blacksmiths and cobblers will often have a painting by their forge or in their stall. Also their other furniture and ornaments costly and curious. Rich cupboards and porcelain, costly fine cages with birds commonly to be found in houses of the lower class. Few carts or sleds used but great quantities of commodities are brought by water in lighters to their warehouse doors.

For their shipping, traffic and commerce by sea, I conceive no place in the world comes near it. Whilst I was there 26 ships came into the Texel. Eight were from the East Indies, nine from the West Indies and nine from Guinea. By means of their shipping they are plentifully supplied with what the earth affords for the use of man, as corn, pitch, tar, flax, hemp from Danzig and the Baltic Sea; masts, timber and fish from Norway; cattle from Denmark.

Of their public buildings, the Exchange is like that at London. Their hospitals for orphans, sick persons, lame soldiers, old people, mad people etc are fairly built, wonderfully well furnished and cleanly kept. There are two houses of correction. In one the men are put to hard labour: the women and wenches are more favoured in the Spynnehouse for they sit like so many at school, very civilly and quietly at their needle, wanting nothing but liberty. Many of them better in than out.

Their church steeples and clocktowers are from about the middle part upward, of an admirable geometrical and artificial form, commonly of timber carved, with lead: full of arches, pillars, pinnacles, galleries, one above the other, lessening to the top. The bells for the chimes all in sight. The Giralda at Seville resembling these but that is of stone.

The lack of facilities for walking in the country has made these people to countervail it in home delights as in their streets, houses, ornament, furniture, little gardens, flower pots, in which latter are curious and rare plants: incredible prices are paid for tulip roots and for rareties of foreign countries, wherein they take delight.

Here is a great barrel or tun containing about one hundred hogsheads and more: the timber work very strong and neat, with many great iron hoops. It is new and entire, but not now in use except to be seen by visitors and for a drinking room when required, there being a little door to creep in where they must have candlelight. In the middle is a table where eight people may sit aside: a strong, costly and curious piece of work.

I have described this place at some length partly because it differs and at times excels other parts and partly because I have a strong affection for the manner of living in this country.

Of a Voyage from Amsterdam unto Danzig in the Baltic Sea with somewhat of Prussia and the countries adjoining.

17th August 1640. We set sail from Amsterdam in the Hope of Vlieland, skipper William Tiebbes, being a Monday morning and that afternoon ran aground on a mudbank at the entrance to the Zuider Zee but came off again.

26th August. We sailed from the Vlie with a fleet of about 240 sail, whereof twelve were men-of-war for convoy against the Dunkirkers. We passed by divers beacons, towers, seamarks etc and sundry buoys, some white and some black, needful by reason of the dangers of this coast, so full of bankes, shoals and sands. Part of this fleet was bound for Norway, the rest for Danzig and places in the Baltic Sea.

29th August.   About half our fleet left us for Norway whilst we took a more easterly course towards the Sound. This evening we met another fleet, near upon 100 sail bound westward. I never saw a greater fleet in all my life being about 300 vessels under sail.

31st August.   We came and anchored near Elsinore. Here is a fair and sightly castle, by report very strong and strangers not allowed to enter. A great number of ships must here anchor to pay duties unto the King of Denmark. In the town is a lofty church with a fine spire and a fair and costly pulpit. The land about this place very delightful in pretty hillocks and little valleys, pleasant groves of trees and fountains of water. At our inn, which was one of the best, were used no napkins although the service was all rich and cleanly. Also at night we were laid between two featherbeds.

2nd September.   We set sail from Elsinore, having paid 800 rix dollars to clear our ship. As soon as each vessel was visited, she set sail there being now no danger of enemies. At night we anchored off Copenhagen by reason of rocks which were dangerous to be passed at night.

3rd September.   In the morning we saw the city of Copenhagen, about one and a half miles distant. It lies close to the sea with many spires. We passed four of the King of Denmark's ships of war in the roads, not large but very neat. We sailed on past many islands, full of woods and habitations and about noon were out of sight of land. At three o'clock in the afternoon we saw the island of Bornholm.

4th September.   At evening as we were turning into the roads at Danzig, our ship grounded on sand but came presently off again without hurt or danger so that night we anchored before the castle or lighthouse.

5th September.   In the morning the skipper, myself and others went ashore in our boat. Passing the Castle, a large and strongly fortified place, we went about two miles up the river Vistula which is but narrow. So we came to the city of Danzig.

26th September.   I took passage in a smack for Konigsburg. That evening we lay at the Bulwark, two miles below the town at an inn newly built and owned by Mr Thomas Slocombe, an Englishman.

At Konigsberg the Margrave of Brandenburg keeps his court in a large castle in the city. It is larger than Danzig but not so well built or fortified. Here is the greatest trade for oak timber, beams, wainscot, clapboard etc. The piles of timber on either side of the river would take up the space of nearly half a mile square. It cometh down from the country where are vast woods of oak, pine etc. There is also a great store of hemp and flax.

Here is a pretty exchange, finely painted overhead with moral emblems and verses, it stands on the river adjoining a fair bridge which in fine weather serves as part of the exchange. The bridge may be compared to that at Weymouth as well for its use as for its form. I never in my life at one time saw greater flocks of any sort of fowl as here were of wild ducks along the shore. They seemed to fill the air and cover the sea. In winter they repair to England and warmer countries. Also a wonderful number of tame geese between Danzig and Elbing. Many thousands of them are kept for profit, as sheep are with us.

29th September.   I walked up into the country unto a town called Wehlau, some 30 English miles. At the way excellent land, for the most part tilled. I believe that in this country there is seven times as much corn sown and reaped as is eaten by the inhabitants, the rest being shipped to Holland and other countries. Within six miles of Wehlau I returned to Konigsberg and on the way saw great floats or rafts of timber driving down the stream.

24th December.   I departed from Danzig in a waggon towards Thorn. The first half of the way was plain arable land, the other half tillage with woods and lakes.

25th December.   We were on our way about six hours when I felt the greatest cold that ever I did in my life. We were then travelling against the wind which caused my eyes to water and soon I had icicles on my eyelids as big as peas. I tied a cloth over my face but within a little space it became as hard as pasteboard. The cold, meeting with my moist breath caused it to freeze so that it stuck to my moustache and beard and icicles formed near my throat of which I felt the pain long after. My nose was so benumbed that for a while I could not tell whether I had one or not, but it came to itself again though after five or six days all the skin came off. It was a month before I had proper use of one of my fingers. The fault was mine in that being inexperienced I had made no provision, thinking if I could endure the sharpness thereof it were enough. Our meat and drink frozen in the waggon. Great difference between travelling here in winter and in East India in summer yet both bad. Here are strange stories of the effects of cold, having spoken with eye witnesses to some, that some years ago men and women travelling in open waggons were frozen dead, sitting up as though they but slept. Countrymen on sledges laden with wood have been drawn into the market place by their horses when they themselves have been frozen stiff, still holding the reins in their hand. A soldier, standing sentinell with his musket hath been found in that posture stark dead and stiff with cold.

Thorn is a well contrived city and a pleasant place, situated on the river Vistula and walled round, with turrets and nine or ten gates. The best Council house in all this country. In this place and now at this time is kept a great fair, resorted unto from Germany, Italy and Turkey and lasting 15 days. There are many rich and well furnished shops belonging to Scots, there being perhaps a thousand families of that nation resident in this land. Also shops belonging to Armenians, Dutch and French, with a great number of Jews who are permitted at the fair but otherwise not suffered to dwell in the city. Most of their dealings here in furs but they themselves are indifferently dressed because the Poles perhaps would poll them if they made great show of riches.

In these parts there is no labouring in the fields for many months by reason of frost and hard weather, nor no cattle in the field but all housed and fed with hay and straw. A hard winter, as I am told, and which I am now bound to see.

A Journey to Konigsberg over the ice.

29th January.   I departed again towards Konigsberg. As we came forth on to the frozen Vistula, one of the sleds broke through the ice but no hurt.

In this journey we went about 77 miles on the ice, the farther off the shore the better travelling. Speedy, pleasant and easy travelling at present, because of a little frost after a thaw so that the ice is as sleek as glass. Around Danzig I have seen men slide with a wooden invention, having an iron keel, wherewith they will slide away five or six miles in an hour. For ease and speed, sledges traverse this frozen sea as boats do at other times. When we came to the river Pregel, we went about two miles by land, the goods being laden on carts as the river was too bad to sledge on.

Whilst here in Konigsberg I spoke with Mr Walter Rowe, an Englishman who is chief musician to the Marquis of Brandenberg and was friendly entertained. Among his instruments he had one named a barretone, it being a base violl with an addition of many wire strings which run from end to end under the finger board, through the F belly of the instrument which are to be struck with the thumb of the stopping hand: very musical and concordant with the violl, like two instruments at once, the playing on the one being no hindrance to the other. In fine a very fair costly instrument and sweet solemn music.

Great store of deer, hares, wildfowl. At the house where the English attend for divine service in Danzig, was a beast hung up by the heels as tall and bigger than a fair sized horse. It is called an eiland or elk, like a deer, cloven footed but shaggy like a bear. This had no horns.

At Schmergrube I with others walked to the other side of the Naring, about half a mile and came to the open Baltic Sea, not frozen. Here on this beach is gathered great store of yellow amber which is cast forth by the sea, chiefly in summer and found in small pieces among the sand and gravel. Here are sometimes wolves taken but not many. Also bees breed in the boles of pine trees, cherished and looked after by the inhabitants who are mainly fishermen.

I have now and then mentioned crooes or country inns. These give better entertainment than the Khans in Turkey but are not near so good as our English inns. They consist of two large rooms, one being a large stable with two great gates to house horses, waggons and coaches. The other room is called a stube or stove and contains a cackleoven or tiled stove which warms the whole room. The entertainment here consists of bread, beer, aquavite and for bedding, fresh straw at night. Sometimes fresh fish, herrings and butter may be had. At night all lie in common on the floor. At the tables, first come, first served although respect is given to the better sort. In fine better accommodation for horses than for men.

A stove, of which scarcely any house in this country is without, is a principal room which with us is termed a parlour. It is the best furnished room, where the master, his wife and children, and also strangers, do sit, converse, write and pass away their time. In the stove is a fair Cackle oven (Kachelofen) or tiled stove which in the winter is made hot and casteth a heat to the farthest part of the room which must be kept closed so that a little wood will warm a good company, not like our chimney fires. An outer room or hall serves as a kitchen.

A voyage from Danzig unto Archangel in Russia on the White Sea and some small observations of those northern regions.

2nd May 1641 I left Danzig in the ship "Justice" of Lubeck lying in Danzig roads.

3rd May.   We set sail but the winds were contrary and on the 5th we bore back to Hele six miles from Danzig and anchored. Here seals are killed for their skins whereof some are milk-white, while they are young, and growing older become spotted like unto leopards.

9th May.   In the morning we had sight of two cities on the larboard side, Rostock and Holstein. Next day we passed up to the city of Lubeck. This place hath many fair spires and about 12 or 14 ships building on the stocks. A pleasant commodious place, no religion permitted other than Lutheran. Between Lubeck and the town of Oldesloe green and shady woods wherein were store of nightingales singing at all times of the night. That night we stayed at an inn. Here we felt ourselves in some danger as it is said in these inns far from the great highway and lying in the woods, strangers have been made away with, which caused us to keep watch all night, we being so few.

12th May.   We came by road to Hamburg.

17th June, being Thursday I departed from Hamburg and came down to Neumühlen where I went aboard the "St John Evangelist", Hans Shroder master to take my passage to Russia.

25th June.   We were in the latitude of 60 degrees north so that the sun was but four hours under the horizon and no night at all in a manner.

6th July.   At present our midnight being no other than a clear ruddy morning is with us at home. A cold climate though in the heart of summer.

12th July.   In the morning, being clear, we were within four or five miles of the North Cape. Here along the sea coast the inhabitants are Lapps whom I conceive to be the most northern most of all peoples. They fish in winter, the catch being split and dried in the air without salt and then taken in Boats to Bergen as "stockfish". In former times whales were killed at the North Cape.

15th July.   Came a small boat with four Lapps, one a woman, each rowing with two oars. We had from them nearly a hundred-weight of good fresh fish and gave them some biscuit, aqua vitae and tobacco which they rather desired than money. The land near the Cape like our English coast about Cornwall and Devonshire.

18th July.   A great English ship came in.

20th July.   We saw the opposite land, being Russia: thick, dirty, rainy weather.

26th July.   I came up the river Dvina in an English boat. On the way they put ashore to cut a mast for the boat, but coming aboard brought with them a multitude of mosquitoes but by a gale of wind we were cleared of them. That evening we came to the town and castle of St Michael Archangel which makes a handsome show from afar by reason of the many turrets of the churches and castle, all made of wood. Here may be between 25 and 30 sail, six English, five from Hamburg, one from Bremen, one Dane and the rest Hollanders. The English have their Court house apart and most of them dine in common at one table. They enjoy great priviledges and are free of customs. The Dutch have also their house. At this time of the year the Samoyeds repair hither. Clad from head to foot in deerskins, they are very brown, low statured, big-mouthed, small-eyed like Tartars. They eat all manner of trash as guts, garbage etc, sometimes raw, sometimes half roasted. They may keep many wives. They use long bows and arrows tipped with bone. They come first from a country lying far eastward called Samoyeda. They are about a month on the journey, rowing along the shore in small boats. They bring with them to sell live reindeer, very tall, tame, sleek and fair, some almost milk-white. All males and females bear large branched hornes.

The Russian does not permit strangers to enter their churches and allow no carved images. I could not procure one of their pictures (ikons) on any terms, though I begged English and Dutch to send a servant to buy one for me. So much do they reverence pictures. They cross themselves on sundry occasions and not one but wears a cross about his neck.

In August they light their stoves which are in the middle of the room with sundry cupboards adjoining where they keep their provisions and underneath their hens and ducks. The smoke cometh out into the room in which are benches where they sleep on cushions and skins. No beds or chairs. The wealthier people use white tiled stoves, the fire outside and the smoke carried away as at Danzig: so the rooms remain clean and white whereas the others are like a blacksmiths' forge.

There is much business to be done here in a short time: about 30 ships to be unloaded and loaded again; as also the great lighters which come down from the country: all to be done within the space of a month or little more. Also much buying and selling.

The country here yields not much corn, fruit or herbs: yet some corn we saw reaped green and hung up to dry. The summer is as hot as with us but lasteth not much above two months. There is an incredible quantity of the herb and root angelica (archangelica officinalis) and sundry sorts of field flowers and long grass. Of wild swans we saw many hundreds. When the ships depart all the English and Dutch leave and go up into the country mostly to Moscow. Here at present was Mr Thomas Wyche, deputy for the Agent. I knew eight more of his brethren, three in England, three in Turkey, one in Spain, one in East India and now this one in Russia. I served one for two years in Constantinople and another for three years in London. They were the sons of Mr Richard Wyche who had in all eighteen children by the one wife.

The chief commodities are rich furs as black fox and sable brought from Siberia: red hides and elk skins: great store of caviar and for the Mediterranean seaboard cordage, tallow, hemp and train oil from seals. I had a good mind to have gone up to Moscow and was invited thereunto by some of the Englishmen, but this would have required so much time and expense and inconvenience to other business which concerned me, I thought it as well to remain satisfied with what I had seen here and to return by sea. So I agreed with skipper Mathias Paulson of the "Fortune" of Hamburg and we set sail from Archangel on the 2nd September. On the 22nd we passed the North Cape and six days later were off Bergen. The sea water was very green, we now passing between Scotland and Norway.

3rd October.   We saw the island of Heligoland.

5th October.   We left the ship and came to Stade with some passengers bound for Holland.

7th October.   We came to the city of Bremen situated on the river Weser, about 60–70 miles from the sea. A fair prospect from afar, having many churches with high spires covered with copper. Many handsome streets and a strong and complete wall, furnished with many pieces of brass ordnance, some 18 to 20 feet in length.

15th October.   I went to the king of Denmark's camp at Fuhlsbuttel, four miles from Hamburg. It is fortified with a wall of earth, about two miles around wherein lie about 10,000 men their huts of turf and straw in ranks like streets and a store of field ordnance ready mounted on carriages.

16th October.   I departed from Hamburg and next day came to Lubeck, a place of much trade and, by report, 400 ships: they boast they own more shipping than Amsterdam. Much hops grow here and the beer is in great demand and is exported.

24th October.   I departed from Lubeck and next day went aboard the ship "Fortune" of Lubeck and agreed to pay two rix dollars for my passage, with my chest, bedding etc and accommodation in the great Cabin but bringing my own provisions. In two days we safely arrived in Danzig roads, God be praised. On the 1st November I went up to the city, it being almost six months since my departure on this voyage.

Some particulars of the City of Danzig and also my departure thence and arrival home in England once again.

The city of Danzig is under the crown of Poland and reckoned also as part of Prussia. With it's suburbs it may contain a population half as many as Amsterdam or a quarter of that of London. Very hard winters and very hot some part of the summer. It hath some fine streets such as Langmarct, Lang-gast, Yopun-gast, Brede-gast etc with many lofty buildings of brick outwardly adorned with paintings and windows and inwardly costly and curious in furniture, pictures etc. Many rich merchants and shopkeepers, the younger proud and wearing costly apparel so that with the rich eating and drinking, sumptuary laws were brought in by the authorities in 1642 to curb this excess.

For their religion, here are Lutherans, Calvinists and Papists. St

Marys, the principal church is not much smaller than St Paul's in London. It has many great bells, the largest called the Bedeclocke or prayer bell. Some poor blind men take it in turn to ring the bells and there is also a watch maintained all night to look out for fires. From ten o'clock to four at every half hour, the watch play upon hautboys or pipes: four or five pairs of organs, one very large.

The city has a complete wall and a ditch or moat full of water. At the upper end of the Yopun-gast standeth a fine building called the Zeughaus or Munition House. On one floor stand 120 good brass pieces of ordnance, brightly burnished, mounted on strong carriages in ranks with the shot, worms, spunges lying by them. There were also sundry halls with armour and weapons for thousands of men. There were some pretty curiosities including the images of a couple of soldiers life size and in good postures, the one presenting his gun, the other with a drawn sword and buckler. By turning a screw, one gives fire with a loud report and the other brandishes his weapons, their eyes turning with fierce countenances.

The executioner differs much from those in other countries. He is called the Sharp Righter and puts into effect the sentence which the Righter or Judge has imposed. The present official is a handsome man, well apparelled: in winter with a sable cap, plus cloak and sword – a genteel kind of fellow who keeps company with burgers and other men of quality in the best taverns and keeps his own coach and saddle horses.

In winter the people ride in small sledges drawn by one horse called yagh sleds, so called may be from yagh, a swift sailing boat, there being a resemblance between the swift gliding of the one through water and the other speedily sliding over the ice. In these sledges they go with great speed each striving to outgo the other and to get for himself the swiftest paced nag. They use also shooting exercises with crossbows at a fowl made of wood set up on a high pole; also with guns at marks, somewhat like our Military garden in England. Here is fencing, baiting and fighting of beasts as bull, bear and dogs. At the Junkerhof, a large spacious lofty room, well adorned with ancient paintings and rareties, when not used for public meetings or as a court of justice, there is feasting and drinking and in foul weather it is also used as the Exchange.

In the said house are certain free brotherhoods of the principal inhabitants who invite some English and Scots into their company. At certain times these hold frolic feasts at night where is lusty cheer, good wine and beer, with the music of organs, violls and voices. Solemn healths are drunk all round and there is much civil mirth. The room is lit by a great number of wax torches and candles and these feasts might well become the entertainment of an ambassador or prince. Thus cold countries invite men to devise means to come together to cherish and warm themselves.

Some summers our English players and comedians come here and perform, having come from Konigsberg where they performed before the prince elector of Brandenburg and from Warsaw before the King of Poland. Among these actors was one nicknamed Pickled Herring, admired for his dexterity in the jester's part. It is said he could so control his countenance that to one half of the people he would seem heartily to laugh and to those on the other side bitterly to weep and shed tears – strange!

The main trade here is for grain – wheat, barley and rye – brought down the river Weichsel in great flat bottomed lighters. By report above 160,000 tons of corn is shipped from here every summer. The poor people that come down with it are no better than slaves. So great a difference make they in Poland between the gentry and common sort that if one of the latter is killed, they pay but half a crown to the king and are freed. Such oppression is used in most parts of the world in various degrees. Where is it not that poor men must labour, sweat and fare hard to maintain the pride and luxurious living of a few?

The English staple is also kept here: a great company of merchants, factors etc. Many married and living here permanently, having a preacher and a church wherein to hear God's word.

In front of the Junkerhof is a very fair large artificial fountain. The upper part is a Neptune of fine proportions striding seahorses cast in metal. Water is spouted through sundry passages. The clocktower adjoining hath very good chimes. Here also is a very great house containing 18 grinding mills and a house of correction where misgoverned people of both sexes are put to work, spinning and weaving.

An unusual custom here is that poor scholars and blind people sing up and down the streets for alms. I have seen and heard three

or four poor blind fellows, doubtless instructed and taught, with
one to lead them singing so harmoniously as to give much delight
to the hearers.

I forgot the organs in the parish church which deserve notice.
They have, by the report of the chief organist, Paul Eevers, 3256
pipes of various sizes, the biggest of them 2 feet in diameter or six
feet around as I also measured. It hath 54 registers to multiply,
diminish, 24 great bellows blown by four men with their feet.

Warsaw

Here at present was held a Reichstag or assembly of the nobles
about the state of affairs. It was held in a great hall of the king's
palace, the king sitting under a canopy in a chair with a bearskin
under his feet. There is a guard at the door yet almost any man may
come in.

At certain times the nobles attend the palace with great pomp,
each in his coach which are very large, with glass windows, a
couple of bodyguards standing upon the hinder part of the coach,
some of his gentlemen and officers riding before and a company of
his bodyguard following in their livery of one colour with little felt
caps and sabres, back swords, poleaxes and guns.

The nobles in their dress much resemble the Turks in fashion
and colour, as red, green, blue and yellow: fur caps summer and
winter, sometimes with a single feather.

These Reichstags last little more than a fortnight and each lord
then departs to his home where he lives and rules like a little king.
But for the common sort of people, they are miserable like slaves
or beasts, allowed only enough to keep them alive and continue
their labour.

The King is served and attended by strangers – French, Italians
and Germans, some of them of exquisite skill in architecture,
painting and music of which I saw and heard somewhat.

Among persons of dignity here at present: imprimis the king
(Vladislaus IV, 1632–1648): then the queen, sister to the emperor
of Germany: prince Casimir, the king's brother: the bishop of
Cracow, and other noblemen and ladies.

1st April 1643.   I and other good friends took passage in a kahn
or boat to come down to Danzig by water to Palschau and thence
by land.

On our arrival at Danzig there was such a hard frost that some of our Dutch guests went skating alongside the ships in harbour.

Last days in Danzig

On the 10th February 1646 came Madame de Nevers, a great lady of France to be married to the King of Poland whose first wife had died two years before. The city welcomed her with magnificent banquets and presents, and with dancing and fireworks.

In 1646 and 1647 come hither English tumblers who would leap clear over eight, sometimes nine and ten, tall men standing upright, also over sundry pairs of swords and through a hoop: also dancing on a rope in complete armour, the like never yet having been performed.

Whilst I was in Danzig, I went to Braunsberg, a small city where at Shrovetide is held a running tilt, not in such courtly manner as we read in former times to have been performed by lords and knights, for this was done by labourers and country men in a rustic manner. The champions have for their good endeavours a barel or two of strong beer and then visit the burger's daughters in the Junkerhof with whom they dance to the music. Good plain mirth enough.

Having spent almost seven years and to and fro, much of it against my will, yet with an ill-will must I leave this place by reason of the troubles in England (the Civil War) which were not yet stilled. However, occasions compelled me to leave these parts and return home.

A voyage from Danzig to England

We left Danzig on the 28th July 1647 aboard the ship "Prophet Daniel" of Lubeck.

6th August.   We had a fair wind and came as far as the island of Bornholm.

7th August.   Wind came westerly so we anchored on the east side of the island before a town called Tlexö. Here the people came out to us in small yawls with fish, sheep and hens.

11th August.   About noon we arrived before Copenhagen. About a mile from the shore we saw two floating castles of the

King of Denmark which he caused to be made to prevent the passage of the Sound in the last invasion of the Swedes: but they hindered not the Hollanders who joined with the Swedes against him in 1643. About three or four of the clock we came near Hven, a pretty little island about a mile in length. Here the late famous astronomer Tycho Brahe had his residence (and observatory).

19th August.   It proving calm the crew went to fish for cod on a reef after a way I saw not before. They have a piece of lead cast in the form of a herring with a double hook attached, which, being let down to the bottom, they suddenly and violently snatch up again. This they do continually. The live fish do not bite the bait but are caught on the attached hooks. We caught no cod but instead a pretty store of mackerel which are usually caught in a gale of wind when the boat is well under way.

23rd August.   We saw a couple of herring busses bound Eastward.

24th August.   We met two handsome well appointed Scottish ships and a Hollander.

25th August.   This morning we sailed along the (English) shore: fair wind and weather. Many fine towns in sight as Yarmouth, Lowestoft, Southwold, Dunwich and Aldeburgh. Hardly a seashore to be seen better stored with towns, trees and tillage than was this, but on the other hand not a more dangerous coast for shoals and banks.

27th August.   We came to Gravesend where we took boat to London and landed at Billingsgate, I being just 50 years of age. Here we found a great and strange alteration in city and country, in the religion, government and affections of the people but of these confusions I am not able to judge.

5th October.   We left London for Gravesend but our ship, the "Morning Star" had sailed three or four hours before, so we hired a barge to overtake her and next morning found her at anchor in the Downs and went aboard.

16th October.   At night we arrived in Plymouth Sound.

17th October.   We came into Cattewater. Here we saw tokens of our Civil War, as in some places new fortifications and in others ruins of houses.

18th October.   We set sail in a small bark.

19th October.   In the morning we arrived in the harbour of

Falmouth once again, here making an end of a most tedious, troublesome and costly voyage and the worst of the many in this book. God's name be praised for our safe arrival and send us an end to these general troubles, as also to my own particular ones and give us all grace to better our lives.

Costumes seen at Danzig – some of Peter Mundy's own sketches.

CHAPTER VIII

Of the County of Cornwall and the Towne of Penrinn

1650

I will now touch particularly at the county of Cornwall and towne of Penrin, the place of my nativity, por amor de la Patria.

Cornwall is the westernmost county of all England, and in it the Lizard, (a cape or headland well knowen by seamen) lying in 50 degrees 10 minutts north latitude.

They have a speech peculier to themselves, somewhatt agreeing with Welsh and that used in Little Brittany in France, and by the opinion of the learned is the relicque of the language of the ancient Brittaines inhabiting this Ile who by sundry invasions were faine to withdraw themselves among the mountaines of Wales and hilly country of Cornwall and some over into France, which part is called Brittany. But now that speech with us is much worne outt and English spoken over all, which by report is as good as any in England, especially at and near the seaports.

This county is in compasse about 190 miles, viz 40 miles by land from the north shore by Ham unto Rame Head by Plimmuth on the south are about 40 miles, the river Tamar dividing it from Devonshire, making it almost an island, for it hath its beginning not four miles from the North Sea (i.e. Bristol Channel), and passing by Saltash, runneth into the south by Plimmouth; only North Petherwin is accounted in Devonshire, although it lies on the west side of the river, where I lived awhile with my uncle Mr John Jackson, who married my father's sister. He was preacher and pastor of that parish about 1608. From Rame Head unto the Lands End is by sea near 70 miles and from thence again to Ham about 80, so that the shore of this county is washed with the sea near the space of 150 miles, which is more than any other shore in England.

It hath sundry good havens on the south, as Falmouth, Hailford (Helford), Foy (Fowey) etc. Falmouth is famous for harbouring of shipping either outward or homeward. It may be accounted the second in England, if not the first (as you may read in Speed's Chronicle) within which 100 sail of ships may ride and the one not see the other from their main tops, the harbour divided into so many creeks and branches. Some say the rock at the coming in, commonly called the Black Rock is named Falmouth and that from it the harbour takes its name, but more probable from the river Vale (Fal) beginning near Roche, passing by Granpont (Grampound) and Tregony and so into the harbour at Talverne (Tolvern) passage.

On the starboard side coming in, standeth St Mawes Castle situated low and near the waterside. But on the larboard side standeth Pendennis Castle mounted on the top of a hill or peninsula (for it is almost an island). Toward the waterside coming in is a blockhouse, and below that a complete platform furnished with good ordnance. This Castle is become famous nowadaies. It is about 2½ miles from Penrin and many wish it were farther off in these tymes, anno 1650.

The country is general hilly, with many large downs but within these (last) few years the inhabitants have much improved the ground (and do still go on) especially near towns. Penrin may be an example: the eastward brought to tillage and most of the west, besides making enclosures from the downs. It is generally well supplied with water, as running brooks, rillets, well springs. As however the soil is accounted none of the best, yet I dare say that the worst land in Cornwall is as beneficial to the Kingdom as the best ground in England for where is our worst ground, there the tin mines are, which for the most part is moorish, marshy, stony, rocky, heathy, gravelly barren ground from which may be drawn yearly about 400 tons of tin (this in only my computation): most part thereof transported into forraigne parts, much to Constantinople and parts of Turkey, Italy, Spaine, France etc which by the returns yield much benefit to the kingdom besides supplying our own land.

This county affordeth plenty and variety for sustenance of man's life, as corn, cattle, fish, fowl and fruit.

Corn: wheat, barley, oats, rye. There is sometimes sent supplies

82

Chapter VIII

of wheat and grain from hence to London. Also many ships putting into our harbours are supplied with biskit, beere, beef, pork and butter.

Cattle: bullocks, hogs and sheep which yieldeth good beef, pork and mutton, which although not so great in general as about London, yet not inferior in goodness and sweetness. With these ships outward bound do make provision.

Fish: first the pilchard, which although one of the least (in size) yet deserves the first rank, not only for the goodness of the fish itself, being white, solid and of a pleasant smacke (flavour) but for the great benefit it bringeth to the whole land: for I conceive (it is but my judgement only) there may be 5 or 6 thousand tons yearly transported to France, Spaine, Portugall, Italy, producing returns from thence in gold, silver, wines, oil, fruit, iron, wood etc. besides the country around being suplied, it being a great help to the poorer sort. They are termed by most dealers fuinados, because in former times they hung them in smoke but now, and for many years since, they press them, making good benefit of the train oil.

Then conger, very big and long: some near 20 inches about and 6 or 7 inches through. Excellent fresh cod, ling, hake (the forerunner of the pilchard) haddock, bream, chads (nicknamed choake children) and scads. Whiting all the year. Sometimes bass and great mullets, as big as I have seen elsewhere: Gurnards, grey and red, turbot, great soles and plaice; wrathes (wrasse) smelts, mackerel and murghee (dogfish) which although of no great esteem yet to my mind, being well baked in a pan with good wholesome herbs, butter, pepper and salt) is as good as the best thorneback; ray, surmilletts (red mullet) and other.

I will only mention one more, viz. I was once a fishing with others about Milerstone (Mylor) a little below Parckhellen where we drew ashore a slender fish like a gherricke (three bearded rockling) about a foot long. It had two venters, or bellys, one under another, the uppermost for the entrails, close as in other fishes, and another, under that, open which did close with two lappets, wherein she bred her young, for there were in it a multitude of small ones. This creature in the sea imitates in that particular, another on land, viz an opossum, a four footed beast in the West Indies (i.e. New World) of which I have read and heard but never saw. This fish by the common people is termed a sea-adder (pipe fish). There are also fresh water eels taken in the channel that runneth from the town when the tide is out, and plaice which they find by treading, as they wade along.

Now a word or two of shellfish. Lobsters, much esteemed in some parts with us, cheap because plentiful, at 1d, 1½d or 2d a piece at most; of which are sent to London alone 15 or 16,000 yearly. Longoisters (rock lobster, sea crawfish or langouste), like lobsters but bigger: stoolecrabbs (male edible crab) oysters in abundance from Mopus (Malpas) and other places at 2d or 3d the hundred, many hundred barrels sent from thence to London pickled. But there is a sort gathered near Penrin called barre oysters which for the bigness hath the biggest pulp of any that I saw. Mussels, cockles, limpots (limpets), perriwinckles, which we term winckles. These last four go under the name of treegmeat and are commonly eaten in Lent (sometimes scallops and tienns, a shellfish). Thus much of fish of several sorts to be at several seasons, some all the year, of all which this place is plentifully provided from the grand magazine, the ocean, which with two arms embraceth this county. Even the rocks yield sampeer (samphire) for sauce.

For tame fowl: pheasant, heron, partridge, heathcock (black game) woodcock, snites (snipe) cerlues (curlews). In winter wild geese, wild ducks, blackbirds, thrush, velvares (fieldfare) wheenards (redwing). From the sea, shag, barregander (sheldrake) and about Scilly – pewitts (blackbacked gulls). I had almost forgot the Cornish daw, so called because in a matter peculiar to that county, breeding in shafts or tin pits, seldom seen elsewhere. It hath a note like a chough, but pleasanter.

Fruits: apples, pears, plums: of such plenty and various sorts so that some years they make great quantity of cider of the overplus of apples growing around our town (Penryn).

Herbs of all sorts, thrift on the rocks, undercliff, underwoodland.

Cornish nags, goonhillies etc. esteemed for their mettle, durableness of travel and hardiness of feeding.

Cornish hair: a certain wool, so termed with us, comparable with the best in England.

Cornish diamonds are of no great consequence.

Recreations

For recreation: hurling and wrastling, generally a manly pastime with vigorous action, performed by a company of choice lusty men who contend who shall carry away the golden ball. Hunting the otter, badger, fox, hare etc. I having been at all these sports. Fowling and hawking.

The county hath other metals, witness the metal works at Twelve Head and leaden mines by Helston.

Penrin

Now somewhat of Penrin in particular. Penrin standeth in latitude 50⅔, somewhat less North and from the Azores about 18½d West, consisting of 150 households more or less which now I will compare to great Constantinople renowned, viz that standeth on many hills, this (Penryn) upon one environed with many... This also is embraced by two arms of the sea, one runneth up by Gluvias Church and the other up by the Summer Court to the Bridge. As in Constantinople the Grand Seigneur's Serraglio or place of pleasure stands on the point that divides them, so we in like manner have a pleasant place for recreation named Parchellan, a fine bowling green and two brooks. The town is surrounded with orchards of fruitfull trees and a wholesome water runs through the middle descending by chutes from one to another besides many excellent springs at a brook at the end of almost every orchard.

At Constantinople are many ancient monuments. Here at Penrin are the ruins of the famous and ancient College of Glasney, the ruins of church and steeple yet to be seen, many strong towers remaining yet entire. If you behold the town from Behellan fields, the High Cross, East and West Wood, it presents as fine a prospect as any town in England, especially in spring and summer although coming into it, you will be disappointed in regard to the uncleaness and uneveness of the streets, in some places unpaved and the benefit of running water through the town not made use of.

The town has a handsome Markethouse on a rising hill. It is governed by a Mayor, of which I saw the first, 12 Aldermen, 12 Assistants, a Recorder, Town Clerk and two serjeants-at-mace. Arms: a Saracen's Head.

Mr Carew saith of Penrin that it is a town rather passable than notable for wealth, building and inhabitants. This was in 1602 but it is now well improved in all three: many wealthy burgesses fair buildings and much more peopled, and may now compare with Truro.

Again he (Carew) saith Glasney College was founded by Walter Browne, beneficed by John Grandison, both bishops of Exeter, the first in 1256, the latter in 1327. I have heard say my grandfather, Peter Mundy was either canon or chanter in that College 120 years since. And so much for our Towne.

A Triumph

Having read of a Roman Triumph, I will now relate of a Cornish Triumph, performed at my being there, to fill up this side (of the paper).

In June 1648 Pensance rose: to suppress whom were sent certain companies under Colonel Bennett, who made short work, killed some, took others prisoner, scattered the rest and plundered the town. The victors passed through our town (Penryn) in a triumphant manner, viz three soldiers, upon the points of three swords carried upright – three silver balls used in hurling. Then followed another three soldiers marching very grandly in Aldermen's gowns, the soldiers marching after with plundered ribbons and favours in their hats, ever and anon shooting off their guns and shouting. Then followed certain horses laden with pillage, as feather beds, household goods etc and before them 40 prisoners. In this manner they marched up St Thomas Street, about the Fish Cross, to the upper end of the town on the lower side of the street and down again. The Triumph being ended, the soldiers repaired to their quarters and the prisoners were committed to the Markethouse.

Among the said prisoners was one Glover who, finding his opportunity, sent his guard going with a box on the ear, took away his musket and escaped; at length he arrived at Scilly and then in a boat with a lusty crew came back to the mainland, landing at Gunwalloe. Marching inland they took prisoner a Mr Sparnon whom they proposed to ransom for £1,000. Unfortunately the prisoner also escaped. Thus to make good the old saying – "Better do something to no purpose than be idle" – having at present spare time.

P.M.

Occurrences since my last arrivall at home 1651–1654.

Three very notable things happened with us since my coming home within these last three years:

1. An earthquake the 25th December 1651, felt in the town and 20 miles about, more or less, about nine of the clock at night, with a groaning noise resembling that of a great turn (spinning wheel) wherewith they spin wool in the country, with a trembling and shuddering motion. It lasted for about a minute.
2. A comet appeared about the middle of December 1652, mentioned in the almanacks of 1653.
3. A monstrous birth. The wife of Thomas Notte, a tanner of our town, delivered of two female children joined together from their throats to the bottom of their bellies 1654.

Penrin the 9th September 1654

We set sail on this day from Falmouth in a small vessel keeping close to the coast. The times being dangerous and our ship not armed, we kept our distance from other ships which seemed hostile but during the night, having made all sail, we lost them.

11th September. We passed by the Needles, between Hurst Castle and the Ilse of Wight as far as Ryde close to some of the pleasantest landscapes that ever I saw, especially two lovely little lowly hills, diapered with delightful fields, meadows, woods, groves, orchards with fruitladen trees; the town lying between both hills but the houses scattered among the trees as in India and Sumatra. The Island very pleasant and plentiful of provisions of all sorts from whence they send supply to the mainland.

12th September. We crossed over to Portsmouth and passed by our fleet, consisting of 13 or 14 sail of stately, stout and warlike ships and frigotts. There being at the time a great impress for men, we were commanded to come alongside the "Marston Moor" frigate but were soon dismissed and allowed to proceed. But when we were about a mile and a half from the ship, we heard the report of a piece of ordnance and the shrill whistling of the shot, it being in its swiftest motion. As this sound abated, the noise became graver and deeper, rattling and tearing in a terrible manner, so that it put me in great fear, for the shot came right over us and in my opinion within nine or ten feet above our heads and a little ahead of the boat. I dare say the gunner for his life could not make a better shot. It came from the "Torrington" frigott, aimed at us to have us return, imagining we had some seamen hidden in our boat. We stopped not but kept on our way to Portsmouth.

A question: Whereas it is commonly supposed that the shot and the report arrive at one instant; we found it otherwise, having heard the report a pretty space before the shot came to us, by computation about 6 or 7 seconds, the shot flying each second near a quarter of a mile: this is somewhat more or less.

Among other things of note here in Portsmouth is the narrowness and depth of the entrance into the harbour between Gosport and Portsmouth. The fair, spacious, commodious and well furnished carpenters' yard for building, rigging, setting forth of ships (as yet no dry dock) having lately launched one called the "Lime" (Lyme) frigott, a very gallant and comely vessel, as yet unrigged: her head and stern richly carved and gilt; her ports had a gold list or edging round about: burthen about 600 tons. To be noted: that "Lime" (Lyme), "Marston Moor", "Torrington" are names and places given in these days to shipping in remembrance of some great and notable victories obtained in such places, and otherwise of harbours as "Portsmouth", frigott and "Falmouth", frigott.

14th September. We departed from Portsmouth, it being a garrison town on a waggon for London, paying 5 shillings per person and 4 shillings per cwt of goods. That night we came to Petersfield (14 miles): the next night to Godalming (16 miles) a pretty big town seated on a rising hill near a fine river (Wey) with many fair meadows. Here is much wire drawn. The third day we passed by Guildford, a fair large country town, Ditton and Kingston (12 miles) a very fair and ancient town and so to London (Southwark) a very woody country for the most part.

The seal of the towne of Penrin (see page 84)

CHAPTER IX

Third Voyage to India
1655 to 1657

Having had sundry crosses, losses, hinderances and discontents at home by bankrupts, repairing of ruined houses, redeeming land sold, paying old debts (none of mine own) I determined to seek some imploiment abroad, so was offered employment to proceed to India as an assistant to the Worshipfull Edward Knipe on the ship Alleppo Merchant.

The 8th March anno 1655 I went aboard of our ship Alleppo Merchant, lying at Woolwich: from whence went ashoare and aboard the State's stately ship the Naseby, lying there in the dark almost finished; she is incomparable for form, exquisitely contrived within and without, curiously carved and richly guilt; her cabins exceedingly spacious and beautiful in painting, guilding and carving; her side galleries being taken into the cabins which serve for very faire windowes, giving great light and adding great beauty to the rooms. Her beake (figure) head is an armed man on horseback with a pistol in his right hand and a sword in his left, with the images of three men lying grovelling under his horse's belly, which by some is interpreted my Lord Protector triumphing over three kingdoms. The English, Scottish and Irish.

The ship deserves admiration, yielding unto the beholders a very gallant and pleasant sight. She is by the keel 132 feet in length. The table under the half deck for the officers 25 feet in length, with turned stanchions on both sides, as was usual in the great East India ships in former times. Her masts of one tree; the main mast being 38 inches in diameter, brought from New England. There are 70 pieces of brass ordnance, great and small, cast purposely for her.

9th March. Aboard our ship, the Alleppo Merchant, a pretty young man being on the main stay and thinking to lower himself by a tackle fastened to a guy rope, most unfortunately mistook, laying hold of the standing part instead of the other, so that he fell into the hold of the ship. I saw him falling with exceeding swiftness and heard the violent rattling of the shiver (pulley). With the fall he lay dead for a while, but the mariners recovered life in him. However, his thigh was broken, so was carried ashored to be cured. The young man's name was John Richardson, a pretty active, well qualified youth.

13th March.   The ship fell down to Gravesend.

15th March.   I came aboard with my apparel and heavy baggage.

17th March.   The men received their imprest money (advance pay) and entered into the whole pay.

20th March.   There fell out another unhappy accident by our ship's side. £2,000 sterling in gold overturned by the Custom House guards through want of proper care (original in Spanish).

25th March.   We set saile in the morning and about two in the afternoon anchored before the town of Margate, about a league short of the North Foreland.

3rd April.   We wayed (anchor) and sett saile from the Downs, being five ships in consort, viz the "Alleppo Merchant", capt. Nicholas Millett; the "Rose", frigate, our pinnace, Mr Robert Nash; the "Constantinople Merchant", captain Browne; the "Imployment", capt. Dibbs; and the "Adventure", capt. Benn, all bound for India.

6th April.   We were in sight of the Lizard and passed by it.

13th April.   We had the wind somewhat better, but it blew very hard with a growne (swollen) sea.

19th April.   We had sight of the Grand Canaries: that night we passed between it and Fuerteventura.

20th April.   We had yet sight of the Canaries astern of us. That morning, capt. Browne in the "Constantinople Merchant" saluted us with three pieces of ordnance, took his leave and his best advantage, setting all his sails to prosecute his voyage, being a far better sailor than we were. Contrariwise capt. Benn in the "Adventure", a bad sailor, of whom we lost sight before morning, leaving her astern.

21st April.   At three of the clock in the afternoon we crossed the Tropicke of Cancer.

22nd April.   This afternoon Capt. Dibbs in the "Imployment" saluted us also with three guns, took his leave and proceeded on his imploiment. We answered him with one. So now we remain in company of our "Rose" only.

23rd April.   At night we set a light at our bowsprit's end which is a gentle check to such ships as run ahead of their Admiral in the night. It was for the "Rose". I have set it downe because others may know the custom of the sea in such cases, it being the first time I saw it.

28th April.   The "Rose's" company took divers tortoises (turtles). They brought us three or four. They are savoury meat. Twelve pieces of ordnance and four anchors stored down in the hold.

15th April.   We reached the Equator.

May 1655.   These five or six days – calms, little wind hot and moist weather.

31st May.   We crossed the Tropicke of Capricorne.

2nd June.   Yesterday and today we saw pintados (Cape pigeons) a sea fowl held by some to be one of the signs of being near the Cape of Good Hope. But we found it otherwise, we wanting as yet thither about 800 leagues.

10th June.   We struck three great dolphins with a fish guig (harpoon), the biggest 61 inches long. It excels for goodness and sweetness in taste.

27th June.   Sudden gusts. We saw certain great fowl called alcatrazes (albatrosses) not much different from our great grey gulls in the West Country, but these are exceeding long winged.

28th July.   We had sight of the great island of Madagascar.

3rd August.   This morning we saw a small island before us, not set down in our ordinary charts, although the Master had it in his. There we saw a ship close to the shore whom we supposed to be aground. After a while she set sail and we met her at the west end of the island. It was the "Constantinople Merchant" who yesterday morning very early ran ashore on the island on a coral bank. To lighten the ship, they threw over board seven pieces of ordnance, five butts of sack, seven butts of beer etc and so came off, leaving two anchors, and cables behind. It was very fair and somewhat still weather, otherwise she had undoubtedly been lost. We named it Christopher Island after Mr Knipe's youngest son.

Mr Haithon, our Master's mate with a fish guig caught a small

The Cape of Good Hope, 1652

tortoise called a hawksbill tortoise. They are of the sort that affords the precious shell wherewith rich cabinets, combs etc are made. It was very good meat.

7th August. We saw the islands of Mohilla and Johanna. Mr Knipe with his three Assistants, Mr Charles Goldsmith, Mr Edward Pate and myself in the afternoon went on board the "Rose" frigate to get into Johanna to trim and fit her to proceed to Surat before the "Alleppo Merchant" in order to further our employers' affairs. Today we saw the other two islands, Moyotas and Comoro. We had calmes and little wind until we came in, helping ourselves with long oars which the frigate brought for such occasions. We came to Johanna and anchored about half a mile from the west town before a valley wherein was a grove of coco trees, plantains etc, called by the English Captain Brown's (Lemon) Garden.

15th August. The "Alleppo Merchant" arrived and anchored by us.

16th August. We went up with Mr Knipe about two miles from the town to visit his old host Abdulla where he found entertainment at such time as he and 22 more were left ashore by Captain Mucknell in the "John", anno 1645 outward bound for India, when he returned with the ship to England, and putting into Bristol, delivered her up with treasure and goods to the King. There might be aloft on the hill about 200 houses dispersed in sundry villages made of cajans, or the leaves of the coco trees, prettily woven and contrived. The said leaves are about 18 to 20 feet long, and durable. Their water they fetch from the river a mile off in great gourds or calabashes containing up to eight gallons.

17th August. The "Adventure", captain Taylor, came into the roads and anchored by us: she had been at Mozambique for ten days.

18th August. The "Rose" frigate set sail for Surat. On her went Mr Charles Goldsmith with orders and instructions touching our Company's business.

22nd August. Johanna is very high land and uneven for the most part, and some exceeding high mountains, yet all generally wonderful fertile from the tops of the highest hills to the bottom of the lowest valleys, the earth a fine mould, the trees always green; abundantly supplied with brooks and rivulets of fresh water. A place of good refreshment for ships, affording good bullocks at 2–4 Spanish dollars a piece, goats from ½ to 1 dollar, the meat nothing inferior to our mutton; cocks and hens 10 or 12 for 1 dollar. Moreover, coconuts, plantains, rice, cuscus, oranges, limes (sweet) potatoes, ananasses or pine apples; a small sort of orange called by us China oranges cangas or guinea hens. The coco tree affords great sustenance to the inhabitants, their cattle and poultry, as also materials to build their houses.

Here are monkeys and another animal called by us a bugee (collared lemur). It hath a sharp muzzle, a very long tail, a very soft and thick fur, the hinder part of his body much higher than the forepart. It had the foremost part of the hinder feet unproportionately big like thumbs. It was exceedingly nimble and would skip from rope to rope, topmost stays and uppermost lines of the ship with such agility that it seemed rather to fly than to leap. And so familiar to everyone that he would leap on their shoulders, take them fast about their necks and lick their mouths and faces. It died on the way homeward.

28th August. We met a junk and took from her 54 slaves.

31st August. We crossed the Equator.

23rd September. The sight of land in 19½ fathom. This evening we saw three sail which we imagined to be Malabar frigates, pirates lying here to meet with Gujerat junks coming from the Red Sea. This evening also we saw land.

26th September. The "Constantinople Merchant" came in from Swally Hole (or Port Swally) where she arrived three weeks since. She touched not at the islands for refreshing so that eight men died and after her arrival here more forsooke the ship: now bound for Rajapore.

28th September. We weighed (anchor) and bent our course for Rajapore.

30th September. We anchored before Damaon, a place of the Portugalls, a very pretty and strong garrison town by report of those that went on shore for I went not, being taken very ill with the flux (dysentery) and a fever.

10th October. We anchored in Rajapore Roads.

11th October. The "Rose" set sail for Goa. We had brought aboard of us, very good fish like unto bonitos but wrought on the back like mackerall. They also had in their boats shovell (probably hammer) nosed sharks but we bought none of them. This place is under the King of Viziapore (Muhammed Adil Shah 1626–1656).

13th October. This morning the "Alleppo Merchant" set sail from Rajapore Roads, Mr Charles Goldsmith and myself being ordered to remain on shore. There was sent up with us one Christopher Scedall, a Prussian of good parts but bad fortune in coming on this voiage. He was sent ashore very sick and myself not much less.

20th October. This night Christopher Scedall died and next day he was buried by the tombs of the English. Here follows a description of native weights, measures and coins. The principal commodities appear to have been pepper (1,000 tons a year produced), saltpetre, gumlacke (lac), turmerick, myrhh and coarse cloth.

24th October. Capt. Henry Benn in the "Adventure Merchant" arrived in the Roads. Here are pilchards taken salted and sold in the bazaar; a small fish in which our countie of Cornwall abounds and from thence many thousand tons are yearly transported to foreign parts. They are like to ours in shape and taste and by the Portugalls called by the same name viz sardinas.

Our house at Rajapore is pleasantly situated on the banks of the river; between it and the house adjoining is a pretty garden with strange trees and rare plants. It stands in a good air and is delightsome for prospects, down to a grove of mango trees in a pleasant spacious meadow and across to the town of Rajapore standing on the side of a hill. It has the sight of all vesels that pass up and down the river and has a view of the Bandar (Custom House).

3rd November. The "Rose" frigate arrived from Goa. Here in the bazaar we saw a Jugghee (voluntary ascetic and beggar) He had nails on his fingers up to 5 inches in length and was fed by his followers. He sat cross-legged with downcast eyes and a steady countenance, with a leopard skin over his knees and his body covered with ashes. Here are many wild monkeys so tame that they will come into the houses and upon the tiles; the houses very low, one little loft at most. Crows also are so tame that they will take the meat out of their dishes. It seems the people refrain from killing or hurting living creatures. Great store of small parrots; also tigers and leopards which by night come into the streets and

East India Company factory

houses – on the 12th November one killed a couple of bullocks. Here are also very large bats as in most parts of India which are near four feet from the ends of their wings, being stretched out (flying fox or fruit bat). Here is a weed that beareth a hard knobbe, with a flower on it, called in Cornish Pedri Praunter.

14th November. We went above a mile above the town, crossed over the river by boat and came to a hot bath. It runs with a good stream in a stone gutter (like our shoots in Penryn) into a little tank; the water in my opinion as hot (if not hotter) as that of the Bath by Bristol. It lies near the waterside among mango trees.

In our way we saw many thousands of large fair oxen. In the front of the laden oxen were some of the goodliest, extraordinarily garnished and adorned with bells, bosses, cowtails etc on their breasts, heads and horns as in England we use to set the front horses of hackney coaches, wagons etc.

17th November. Capt. Taylor seized a Malabar junk which came in the river to trade but the Governor and local people being discontented thereat and obstructing our business, she was released. The Malabars are our mortal enemies in these parts, being many of them pirates.

18th November. We went to see some superstitious ceremonies in Rajapore in a small pagoda. About this time a woman burned herself alive with her dead husband. This I saw not.

20th November. The "Alleppo Merchant" returned from Goa, having buried since her departure, Mr William Raven, master's mate, a proper able seaman and William Tring, a pretty ingenious boy. All availes not.

6th December. The "Rose" frigate despatched to Banda a port 17 leagues to the south of this place. The nearest mart town is Deechoulee, some 12 leagues up a river. Mr Pate went in her to make an investment in pepper and saltpetre.

22nd December. I found a living scorpion in the inside of my waistcoat as I was going to put it on.

It was of a greyish colour: it had six joints in the tail, at the end whereof was a small crooked and sharp pointed prick with which it wounds and envenoms. It has six feet and two claws like a crab. I set this down, not for any great wonder or danger but rather for the satisfaction of some who have read or heard of scorpions but never saw none.

23rd December. The "Rose" frigate came from Banda and after some trouble brought 30 tons of saltpetre and about 4 or 5 tons of pepper.

30th December. This evening we came down from Rajapore and at night went aboard the "Alleppo Merchant". Eleven persons have died out of that ship since I have been on shore, viz. the master's mate, the master carpenter and his mate, with his boy, a quarter master and a boatswain's mate. The "Rose" has lost an equal number. A word or two more of Rajapore ere we part hence. It lyeth about 20 miles up a big river where a ship of 1000 tons may anchor at high water. There are many vessels like unto galleys owned in the port and these trade to the Gulf of Persia, the Red Sea and south to Macassar. The town has a substantial stone bridge and contains about 1400 houses of one storey. There are 10 or 12 Moslem mosques and an equal number of Hindu temples. There is good provision for food to be had and a plentiful bazaar for rice, butter, spice, sugar and dried fruits from other countries, as dates, almonds etc. At the time of our stay, our fare mainly consisted of chicken in curry and meat and fowl boiled with rice and spices. For drink we had good water, arrack, sugar and limes and at certain times of the year Persian or Shiroz wine which was rather expensive.

31st December. About eight of the clock in the morning we set sail from Rajapore Roads homeward bound.

2nd January 1656. This morning, about two of the clock it was my chance to rise and saw the moon eclipsed, the part to the westward of a dark red. I reckoned that at Falmouth it would have been seen at nine at night on the 1st January.

8th January. We arrived in Port Swally. I found some alteration since I was last here in February 1633. The President's tent being moved to higher ground; a spacious place enclosed wherein are courts, yards, warehouses, etc with elevated rooms fairly built of brick, timber etc to sit, eat, drink and take the air, covered with tiles. The bazaar has also been rebuilt with a handsome row of shops, also tiled. Of Indians of old acquaintance I met some, as Hirgee, Sumgee, Tapidos who were Baruans: merchants and brokers as Nannabey and Coregee but of our English nation but one – then a very civil, affable and industrious lad but now through his long service and good deserts atained unto the highest pitch of preferment. Thus it pleases God to raise up some and throw down others. In fine the old East Indies Company's servants live here in a gentle manner, all business discreetly regulated with moderation much different from the private voiages nowadays, each striving to circumvent another to outbid and outrun one another. But doubtless this confusion will ere long bring forth good order by settling the Old Company again. Here the native merchants begin to be owners of ships, buying them of the English and setting them to sea on their own account.

19th January.   Captain Benn in the "Adventure Merchant", capt. Taylor in the "Adventure" and capt. Browne in the "Constantinople Merchant" set sail for England.

29th January.   This morning we ourselves weighed (anchor) and came out of Port Swally, in company of "Assada Merchant" and anchored at the bar. That evening we shaped our course for England, our native country, where God send us to arrive in safety.

8th February.   The "Asada Merchant" saluted us with three guns, took her leave, bound for Macassar on the Island of Celebes.

20th February.   Today Goodman Michel died, a smith and our armourer, an honest, painstaking, quiet man and a good artificer. He was buried, or thrown into the sea some two or three minutes north of the Equinoctial Line.

23rd February.   This day died Doctor Nathaniel Bernard, our preacher, a learned divine who was one of old King Charles his chaplains, and in these times deprived of all his means. He was but two or three days sick without any great complaining. The next day he was put in a coffin of dead boards, with weight thereto applied. He had read the burial of the dead, after the old way, three days before to Goodman Michell, and now captain Millett did the like for him.

27th April.   This morning we saw land being a high hill that lyeth between Cape d'Agulhas and Cape Falso. We saw a seal with his hinder feet above water and his head down ward. We saw also near a score of petrels fluttering in our wake, close under our stern. This night very much wind.

16th May.   We crossed the Tropic of Capricorn and this evening four great whales played about our ship near half an hour and then steered their course towards the coast of Africa.

St. Helena in the Nineteenth Century

25th May. Being Whit Sunday, at evening we arrived at St Helena and anchored on the N.W. side. We rode at anchor before Breakneck Valley and when we came on shore we found the hills barren, dry and rocky and the ascent exceeding steep, which gave occasion for that name (Breakneck). This put me in mind of a place of that name in English, but in Cornish, our country (native) speech it is called Crack a godua, near our town of Penryn where sometimes they hunt and take both fox and grey brock or badger, but this is at least ten times higher than that. We proceeded leisurely ascending till we came to a pretty valley named Palace Green. Here were many fine springs and many lemon trees, also many cottages built of boughs by those who were lately here before (i.e. Dutch and English sailors).

Being set on shore near Chapel Valley as I went along the beach, I saw a strange creature lying there and perceived that it was alive. It was very weak and hurt in divers places. However when I touched it, it raised its forepart, gaping on me with his wide and terrible jaws. It had the colour and terrible countenance of a lion, with four great teeth (probably a Southern Elephant seal).

We looked for letters but found none, only a great stone at one end of a grave whereon it was mentioned that capt. Henry Benn, commander of the "Adventure Merchant" deceased the 24th April 1656 who was there buried by which we understood that some of our friends had been there.

31st May. Saturday evening we set sail from St. Helena.

7th June. At evening we arrived at Ascension. The most desolate barren land (and like a land that God had cursed) that ever my eyes beheld (worse than Kerne Ky [Carnkie, near Redruth] in Cornwall. Some of our company brought down six or seven goats, doubtless at first left there by the Portugalls; also half a dozen of a strange kind of fowl, much bigger than our starlings: colour grey or dappled, white and black feathers intermixed, eyes like rubies, wings very imperfect so that they cannot raise themselves from the ground. They were taken running, in which they are exceeding swift, helping themselves a little with their wings (as it is said of the ostrich) short billed, cloven footed that can neither fly nor swim. It was more than ordinary dainty meat, relishing like a roasting pig.

(Note: This was a now extinct form of rail, not recorded by any of the other early voyagers].

Here is plenty of good fish to be had and there are many sandy bays and coves where the sea tortoises (turtles) come on shore to lay their eggs which they do at night. We brought aboard five creatures: the substance resembling flesh in appearance and taste. One of them sufficed our whole ship's company for a day. The shell about 4¼ feet long and 3¼ feet wide like a great buckler.

8th June.   This evening, being Sunday, we set sail from Ascension.

15th June.   We met with the ship "William", bound for Surat and from them had notice of open war with Spain and the English Channel crowded with men-of-war, friends and foes. The "William" having been delayed we steered back again with her in company for a while to give time for the writing and delivery of letters on both sides.

2nd July.   We found a leak in our bows but could not come to stop it, so were fain to pull up some of our planks to come to the water which the pump could not reach so we cleared it by bailing from watch to watch.

5th August.   We had sight of nine sail being French vessels from Newfoundland laden with fish, of which they spared us some and kept us company.

Being advised by the "William" of the war with Spain we now prepared for the enemy viz:-

1. We platted our gratings with hoops of iron and fastened them to the deck with iron bars and bolts.
2. We slung our yard arms with iron chains.
3. We put on our waist cloths and top armour and when we saw ships, put out our colours, viz – our ensign on the poop and a pennant at top gallant mast head.
4. Every man appointed to his quarters where he is to remain in the time of the fight.
5. All close boarded cabins, in the cuddy and steerage especially were removed to make room to traverse the ordnance and to manage their arms.
6. Our ordnance, musketts, pistolls, powder and shot, fireworks, pikes, swords etc fitted in readiness.
7. Bulkheads of the steerage, cuddy and cookroom, with their loopholes etc repaired.

8. Tubs of water in several places, including the main top, for quenching of fire.

9. Our chirurgeon was ready with his salves, ointments, rolled bandages, bolsters etc to cure our wounded men.

6th August.   The Lizard seen.

13 August.   We came to Tilbury.

A sad accident ended this (to me) unhappy voyage and with another such it began.

Woolwich 3rd September.   Being ordered to supervise the unlading of the ship and standing then on the upper deck, John Bond, a civil proper young man who had for many years been in India where many of our countrymen were slaughtered by natives and escaped that and other dangers accidentally fell into the hold and was killed.

The "Rose" frigate, our consort when we were outward bound returned from India but within three or four leagues of Scilly was set upon by two Dunkirk privateers and sunk. The master was lost but the rest of her company were saved.

CHAPTER X

Some Occurrences, Passages and Observations since My Last Coming Home

1657 to 1663

London 9th of August 1658. Having leisure and spare paper, I thought it not amiss to set down some accidents that have happened since my last arrival from India to this City, which I have either seen or heard, viz:-

17th February 1656/7. The body of Miles Syndercomb was drawn on a sled to Tower Hill and there buried under the scaffold and a stake plated with iron driven through his body. He was condemned (for treason) to be hanged, drawn and quartered at Tyburn which he prevented by making himself away in such a manner that it was not known how: supposed by snuffing some poisoned powder.

About this time, I say September 4th 1657 the body of Colonel Robert Blake (the late General-at-Sea) was conveyed from Greenwich to Westminster in a barge of state, adorned with mourning scutcheons, standards etc, accompanied with his Highnesses Privy Council, Commissioners of the Admiralty, officers of the Army and Navy, Lord Mayor and Aldermen of the City, with the barges of the several Companies of London, with multitude of lesser vessels covering the river so that I never saw in all my life more at one time in so little compass. In their passage up the river, the ships shot off their ordnance passing by Tower Wharf. There the great guns were discharged and were answered by others on the farthest side of the river and these continued firing until they arrived at Westminster where the corpse was interred in Henry VII's Chapel, at which time the regiments of foot gave several vollies of small shot. I never heard a bigger or better in my life. Thus was he honoured at his death, who had performed such noble service for his country by land and sea in his lifetime. Among other good qualities of this famous commander, it is said he did not regard the company of women, being never married.

About this time came sad tidings from India that Capt. Bayley, commander of the "William" (whom we met under the Line as we came homeward bound) with nine or ten men were drowned in Swally Hole. Coming from the shore at night in the barge, they fell athwart the ship's hawser and were unfortunately overset and all drowned except two or three that caught hold of the long boat astern. Among the rest that perished was one Slade, whose widow Mr Nathaniel Wyche married, he being chosen President for both Surat and Bantam.

3rd June 1658. A whale came up the Thames between Blackwall and Greenwich, where it was killed by the watermen. The like hath not happened in living memory, nor to be found on record. It was 58 feet long, 12 feet high and 14 broad. She had very small eyes which lay very near the ground, one on each side of the head which was different in shape from that of other fishes. She had two holes in the upper part of her head, out of which she spouteth wind and water, which I have often seen at sea. The fins or whale-bones grow in the upper jaw which is enclosed by the lower. It seems to be a young one by the smallness and shortness of the fins.

8th June 1658. Sir Henry Slingsby and Dr Hewitt were beheaded on Tower Hill for treason.

26th June 1658. Certain Quakers burnt several instruments of music, harpsichords, base violls etc on Tower Hill near the scaffold, out of their devotion or barbarism. About the end of this month Dunkirk was taken and handed over to the English.

7th August 1658. I went to see the trial of two mortar pieces in Hackney Marsh.

This spring came an ambassador from Florida in America, said to be brother to a King in that country. The ship that brought him over was cast away near Weymouth, the rest of his countrymen including an interpreter being drowned. It was gathered that he came to kiss my Lord Protector's hand, to seek his friendship and crave his assistance against the Spaniard. He was well entertained by Capt. Watts on Tower Hill for several months and then sent home in a ship set forth by Capt. Watts. This Floridian was somewhat low of stature, hard favoured, swart coloured, broad mouthed, grim and stern. In London he was handsomely apparelled in our English fashion.

3rd September.   Died His Highness Oliver, Lord Protector of England.

5th September.   Richard his eldest son, was proclaimed in his father's room.

23rd November.   The funerall of the said Lord Protector was performed with great solemnity. First several companies of mourners. After came other mourners, great personages, standards and mighty streamers, silver and gold trumpets, drums intermixed; horses of state, twelve in number each with trappings down to the ground and with black plumes on their heads, besides His Highness' charger with a covering of red velvet, richly embroidered with gold and silver. I never saw a horse more richer and gallanter accoutred.

Lastly came the effigy itself, being placed in a stately chariot drawn with six horses. The streets were railed and lined with red coats from Somerset House to Westminster Abbey. The effigy was placed in Henry VIIs Chapel where it shall remain for a certain time to be seen. Sic transit gloria mundi.

About the end of this month came advice that the Alleppo Merchant was cast away near Padstow in Cornwall. Seven persons perished, including a woman and two children. Some goods were saved, the rest lost with the ship. She was richly laden and came from the Levant. In her I made my last unfortunate voyage from India in 1658, in company with the Rose frigate which was sunk by Dunkirkers near the Isles of Scilly; and this is the end of these two unfortunate ships.

22nd April.   The Parliament was dissolved. Richard, Lord Protector, very quietly put from the place. Many of the Kings houses voted to be sold.

1st July 1659.   A great seizure of horses. The Parliament, Council of State and head officers of the Army feasted by the City.

26th October.   This summer we had news that Shah Jehan, the Great Mogul, whom I often saw, was not dead, as reported last year. Also the loss of sundry East India ships including the "William" near Manilla in sight of her port. The men saved themselves in their boats and arriving on shore, made a little fortification and planted therein six pieces of ordnance but were cut off by the inhabitants; among the rest Mr William, supercargo with whom I was well acquainted in London. He was one of the three that escaped drowning in Swally Hole, having then lost his hat and cloak, yet at length, he, with ships, goods and company, came to their appointed end. We understood likewise that the Tartars had come as far south as Macao and over-run that spacious rich and well governed kingdom of China. Also that the Cape of Good Hope was planted by the Hollanders three or four years since, where they have a strong castle with 160 soldiers, many of them having with them their wives and children; also many Boores (Boers) transported thither with their families, their dwellings dispersed over that pleasant plain lying under the Table (Mountain) which affordeth many sweet herbs. Mr Goldsmith told me that the Hollanders had killed a lion that weighed 6 cwt.

October. About the end of this month General Monk moved in Scotland against whom was sent General Lambert on the 5th November.

5th December. There was a tumult supposed to be raised by the apprentices for a free Parliament against the soldiery, so that Cornhill and Leadenhall Street were full of armed men, horse and foot. Some words passed, distasteful to the soldiers so that some of them fired and killed five or six and wounded others. In this month Pendennis Castle (in Cornwall) was said to have been surprised by Mr Boscawen.

20th December. Several risings of the apprentices and seamen but quickly pacified; the gates at Temple Bar unhung and thrown in the street.

January. About the end of this month General Monk arrived at St Albans. On the 3rd February he arrived in the City with a thousand horse and a thousand foot, taking up his lodgings in Whitehall. The soldiers in Somerset House would not give place until they were given their pay and placed a strong guard of musketeers at the gate and 6 or 7 pieces of ordnance within the court. The newly arrived soldiers formed up in good order outside the House and along the Strand. After promises of pay and some disputes the old soldiers departed by a back way.

16th March. General Monk entertained and feasted by several Companies of London and made a Freeman.

24th March. There was a great flood and overflowing of the Thames so that much land about Lambeth was drowned. Between Limehouse and Blackwall, three or four thousand acres of meadow under water and hundreds of sheep and cattle drowned and they say it will cost more than £20,000 to repair the damage.

6th April. The Lord Monk came up by water from Trinity House in a stately new vessel termed by us a galley, its sails striped blue and white, gallantly set forth with flags and streamers and four little brass guns. She was indeed a pretty vessel like unto a small Portuguese frigate such as they have in the East Indies. My Lord was saluted with ordnance from the Tower at his passing by.

1st May 1660. The House of Lords and Commons voted Charles Stuart, Heir apparent to the Kingdom of England, Scotland and Ireland.

About this time news from India that Mr Nathaniel Wyche died at Surat twelve months ago. I have known the father, old Mr Richard Wyche, 9 of his sons and 3 of his daughters – Richard, Thomas, Peter, George, James, Julius, Edward and Nathaniel – all dead. There were 12 brothers – only Henry remaining – and six sisters, three alive.

8th May. This day King Charles the Second was proclaimed in the City of London, King of Great Britain, France and Ireland with great shouts and acclamations of joy, with ringing of bells, shooting of ordnances and bonfires at night.

29th May. His Majesty made his entrance into the City of London, conducted in great triumph with horse, especially several troops and companies – excellent horses bravely accoutred with rich saddles, arms and costly pistols, the riders richly apparelled with scarfs and feathers – proper men, gallant youths – a whole company in cloth of silver doublets, others in buff leather coats thick laid with gold lace and costly sleeves, four or five hundred citizens in plush jackets and gold chains – a gallant company of foot, being apprentices in white doublets; musketeers, a crew of comely, lively lads. In fine here was manifested the state, flower, glory and goodwill of the City. Then came the King's Majesty riding between his two brothers, the Dukes of York and Gloucester. Before him rode my Lord Monk and my Lord Mayor, bareheaded, with many others. My Lord Mayor carried the sword. Lastly came four regiments of my Lord Monk's, old soldiers in armour, viz. back and belly pieces down to the waist, with headpieces. These with all the rest passed on with their drawn swords, flourishing and brandishing their bright weapons over their heads with incessant shouts and acclamations.

Of spectators I should say 150,000 from Blackheath to Whitehall, the fields, highways and hedges covered with people: the trees laden with boys, the streets thronged, the windows full, some even on the roofs. The bells ring out, the conduits run with wine but not a pistol or musket shot is heard: only from the ships and from Tower Hill the ordnance thundered: at night bonfires ended the days' public triumph.

25th September.   The Princess Royal dowager of Orange, the Lady Mary, the King's sister came up the river to Gravesend in the brigandine. They were saluted with ordnance from the ships as they passed along and with about 70 ordnance from the Tower wharf. It being calm water, spring tide and a fair day, they shot the bridge.

You have read before of great triumph, rejoicing and acclamation. Now follows somewhat of sorrow, grief and lamentation.

9th October.   Twenty-eight prisoners were conveyed in coaches from the Tower to Newgate, guarded with a troop of horse and a company of musketeers. They were of those that were judges of old King Charles: among the rest, Sir Hardress Waller, colonel of Pendennis Castle at my being at home; Mr Hugh Peters, our countryman, whose brother, Thomas Peters, was minister at Mylor and supplied Gluvias (this parish) also: Mr Gregory Clement who was once chief at Agra, with whom I was well acquainted in the East Indies about 1630. In the throng I lost my lute book which I much valued.

15th October.   Mr John Carew was drawn to execution on a sled drawn by four great horses: he went with a smiling countenance.

16th October.   Mr Hugh Peters and Mr John Cooke drawn from Newgate to Charing Cross. Mr Peters reviled and hooted at, dirt thrown in his face, whooping and hollowing when they put the rope about his neck, and when he was turned off.

December.   In this month stormy weather, southerly wind and rain. The "Assurance" one of the King's ships sunk in the Thames near Woolwich. With four or five others these ships were intended to go to Guinea to find the river Gambia, to plan and fortify and find from whence the gold cometh.

24th December.   Eleven heads were set on London Bridge so

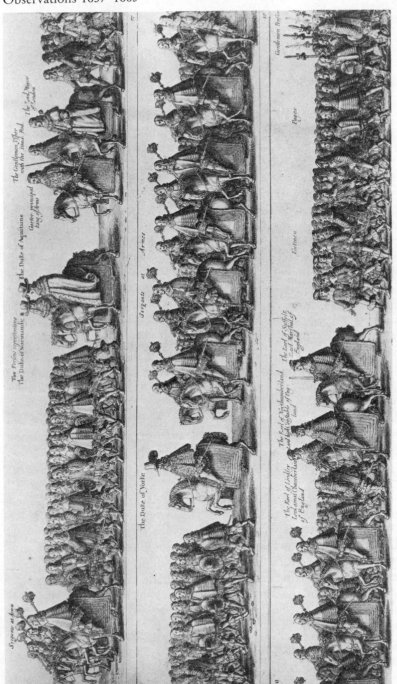

Coronation Procession of Charles II, 1660

that at present there are 21 heads stuck on poles and set over the gate that leadeth unto Southwark.

30th January. The bodies of Cromwell, Ireton and Bradshaw drawn from Westminster to Tyburn and tumbled into one pit under the gallows.

21st April. Mr Richard Jencks died. He had been secretary to the Eastland Company but being fallen into decay in his estate, old and weak in body, he was admitted to the Charterhouse (almshouses) where he died. Not one of the East Country merchants came to his burial. What confidence is to be put in friends. He was a familiar acquaintance of mine.

22nd April. The King's Majesty rode through the City of London in great state passing through several triumphant arches. The East India Company had adorned the front of their house in Leadenhall Street with balconies and overhead a large picture of gallant ships sailing the ocean. The King's Life Guard in bright burnished armour, back and breast with great plumes of red and white feathers. It is to be wondered where so many ostrich feathers could be gotton.

23rd April. The King went to his Coronation on foot, treading on blew broad cloth spread on the ground. The nobles in Parliament robes with gold coronets on their heads marched like so many Kings. The gravest, stateliest and most majestic sight I ever saw.

21st July. Confirmation that the stately ship the Smyrna Merchant with rich varities and strange creatures has been cast away.

26th November. I being at Limehouse saw the "Gold Fleece" launched.

January. We had sad tidings of 15 or 16 sail of our ships taken by pirates of Algiers.

18th February. This morning was such a violent storm of wind which did great hurl in the City, blowing down houses and chimneys which killed many and was likely to blow down my lodging chamber on Tower Hill, the side next the Tower.

April. About the beginning of this month a fleet of ships set sail for East India, including six frigates of the King's to take possession of Bombay.

15th May.   Today the bells rang out for joy for the safe landing of our gracious Queen Catherine at Portsmouth. They had been a month coming from Lisbon and had put in at Scilly.

22nd May.   One Joyce Ebbe was burned alive at Smithfield for killing her husband: a well built handsome young woman of about twenty five apparelled all in white. She gave three or four most loud and lamentable shrieks but presently her breath was stopped with fire and smoke so that in my opinion she was not one minute in pain: it was a sudden alteration from the living body of a young woman to a shovelful of ashes.

About the end of September 1662 at about three or four o'clock in the morning I observed the Pleiades which are certain small stars in the neck of Taurus, the Bull, with a telescope.

March 1663.   About the end of February the "Concord" and "Truro Merchant" arrived from the East Indies and put into Plymouth. The "Truro Merchant" formerly called the "Vivian" sailed from Surat last April and was ten months on her homeward voyage.

Intending, God willing, to repair to my native country, there to end my sinfull and weary days, I think it not amiss (having little else to do) before I leave, to impart some observations. And first of St James Park and the rareties therein:

CHAPTER XI

Home to Cornwall

1663 to 1667

St James' Park

Among my melancholy and solitary walks for divertment (the streets were full of people and much company in the highways yet was I alone) I went sometimes to St James' Park. Since his coming his Majesty hath caused much cost and labour to be bestowed in making it level and taking away many houses built there in these later times.

The Pel Mel, new made, which formerly was in Piccadilly is nearly half a mile in length and a wooden ball may be struck from one end to the other in three or four blows. Lying parallel with it is a new pond of about the same length and about forty yards broad, stored with fish; the water I conceive being drawn from the Thames. There are also nearly a thousand young trees brought from beyond the sea (and called in Danzig "lindenbaum") planted in double ranks, seven or eight yards apart, somewhat like our ash, giving a fine shade and affording a pleasant sight.

Of beasts there were several sorts: an elk, fallow deer, Indian antelopes, spotted deer and a small kind of goat from Guinea. There was abundance of fowl, cranes, storks, spoonbill, pelicans etc. At the beginning of summer the cranes and storks come to Russia and other northern countries where they breed and before winter return with their young to warmer countries again. Peacocks, peahens, a white raven flying to and from the park, a hen with a brood of partridges could also be seen; also outlandish geese and ducks of several shapes, colours and sizes. A great number of our ducks and mallard, widgeon and teal which swim and fly to and fro, frequenting the several ponds. They have little huts or cabins of boards fitted for them to breed.

Between the ponds and Pell Mell there is a mast erected with tackles and pullies for erecting a telescope. The main trunk, made of board lies by it under a shed. This is 35 feet long, so that with the other parts such as lenses, the total length may be 40 feet. Its chief use is to look at the sun, moon, planets and fixed stars.

Near St James' house I saw a cassowary, a strange fowl a little smaller than an ostrich, the body about four feet high and like a turkey and black shining feathers. It hath two feathers in one quill, of which I have some to show. It hath some appearance of wings or pinions, but of no use, as the dodo etc. There was also a she bustard of a fine grey colour as big as a turkey hen.

Greenwich Park

Here are newly planted many young trees. One avenue extends from the Queen's House to the hill where once the castle (or rather the Banquetting House) stood; another avenue on the top of the hill extends a great length eastwards towards Charlton and Woolwich. The side of the hill towards the Queen's House is cut into levels; some of these levels are covered over with green turf and others with gravel.

Blackwall

In the ships carpenters' yard built there long since by the East India Company but since sold by them, there is a new wet dock made with great labour and cost, in circuit about a quarter of a mile and three or four fathoms deep, capable of 25 or 30 ships of the biggest size and intended for ships temporarily out of service. Each ship is fastened with a hawser to the shore and shipkeepers are only required for the prevention of fire. This dock put me in mind of the stately tanks or ponds made with so much art and cost in East India.

20th September 1663. We came from London, taking our passage in the "Goodwill" of Falmouth on a Sunday and on the 27th set sail from the Downs, arriving at Dartmouth the following Wednesday. Dartmouth hath a safe harbour, water enough (at low water) for the biggest ship in England but because it lies in a deep bay and the entrance very narrow, few large ships put in there except bound for or belonging to the port. Whilst we were there, eight or nine good lusty ships, full of men, arrived from Newfoundland. The town affords a fair prospect, the buildings generally covered with slates. A fair church and steeple and the remains of a fair rood loft, curiously carved and richly gilt. On the larboard side of the narrow entrance is a new castle and adjoining the ruins of an old one. On the same side, a little farther in is a small village called Warfleet close to the waterside and near by is the house of Mr Staplehill with a hundred stone steps leading up to it. In this house is much rich furniture and many rareties of nature and art. Some of the furniture was found in the carrack brought in thither in Queen Elizabeth's days taken by us (off the Azores) as she came from the East Indies.

On the other side is a little town called Kingswear with a church in it. Seven miles up lies the ancient town of Totnes where my father was an apprentice. The sea flows up to it.

5th October.   At eight at night the seamen called me up to see three moons: the true moon near the full with two metres or white glares, one on each side. On the Sunday we arrived at Plymouth which is like a small city for fair buildings, fair streets, water conduits, shops and quays: also the pleasant Hoe, the pretty Barbican, the strong Castle (Citadel) and a fair hospital for bringing up poor children. Thus for the land. As for the sea and safety of shipping: the Sound, Catwater, Hamoaze and the haven within the Barbican offer moorings where small and middle sized vessels may safely lie. This place is so convenient and safe for shipping that it is more frequented with Channel shipping than any other coastal harbour whatever the wind. They have also pretty ferryboats for transporting passengers to and fro, with painted backboards, oars and shape like London wherries. Here is a fair church and a lofty steeple; also a fair walk on Catdown.

Falmouth.   We arrived here the 10th October 1663 on which day was a great conjunction of Saturn and Jupiter.

At our arrival we found here three or four hundred French soldiers, half of them in the town and the remainder at Falmouth or Smithick, formerly called Pennycomequick, of which I can remember when there was but one house there. They came here about a month before us, bound for Lisbon and awaiting a Portuguese galleon from Ireland.

22nd January.   The French departed in good order, being for the most part civil proper fellows. They set sail in the galleon escorted by a small English frigate.

8th December.   About five of the clock in the morning myself with others saw a comet in the south, in 175 degrees of right ascension and about 15 degrees south declination. It had been noted by others four or five days since from Pendennis Castle.

1665

This summer, about the beginning of June there was a great seafight between us and the Hollander: a very sharp, fierce and bloody encounter from which both sides came off with great loss. Although we made a kind of rejoicing with bonfires, ringing of bells yet it was supposed by some we had no great cause for it.

There was also great mortality of people in London so that there died of the plague or pestilence about 100,000 persons in a few months: some weeks there died 8 and 9,000.

3rd September. A fire was kindled in Pudding Lane, near Fresh Wharf by London Bridge which increased to such a height of rage and fury, with the help of a strong East wind that it destroyed four score parishes with the churches and dwelling houses ... It burned also underground, for the stationers had filled St Faiths, near St Pauls, with books which were all consumed to ashes; and by report it melted the bells in the steeples.

1667

This summer a fleet of Hollanders come upon our western coast, plying to and fro, eastward and westward and across to the coast of France waiting for our homeward bound ships. But during this time two of our fleets, by Divine Providence, escaped them and arrived safely – the first fleet from the Levant, put into Plymouth and Dartmouth, the other fleet from Barbados and the West Indies, put into Plymouth and Fowey. Seven or eight companies of soldiers were quartered at Penrin and Falmouth at this time.

Now have I done with this sad relation because at the middle of August we had intelligence of a peace concluded at Breda between us, the Dutch and neighbour nations.

From Penrin I began my travells and here I hope to find my haven of rest and ease of all my travells and trouble by that universal remedy (death).

INDEX